CARLA DA COSTA is a creative entrepreneur, business owner, author, divorce coach and leading modern voice on marriage dissolution. Through her private coaching practice, online programs and range of *Divorce Like a Queen* products, she has empowered countless individuals worldwide in financial sovereignty, career, love, relationships and self. Carla guides those who are separated, divorcing, or divorced to make this next season of their life the best season of their life.

Scan the QR code to explore the **Divorce Like a Queen** online shop.

www.divorcelikeaqueen.com

@divorcelikeaqueen

Scan the QR code to discover Carla's **coaching programs and online courses.**

www.carladacosta.com

@carladacostacoach

How to Divorce (and move on) Like a Queen

How to Divorce (and move on) Like a Queen

CARLA DA COSTA

First published by The Kind Press in 2025

Copyright © Carla Da Costa, 2025

Cover design: by Christa Moffitt, Christabella Designs
Cover photo: Ela Amzucu
Typeset in 10/16 pt Greycliff CF by Post Pre-press Group

All rights reserved. No part of this book may be reproduced by any mechanical, photographic or electronic process, including AI-generated reproductions, or in the form of a phonographic recording, nor may it be stored in a retrieval system, transmitted, or otherwise copied for public or private use other than for 'fair use' as brief quotations embodied in articles and reviews without prior written permission from the publisher.

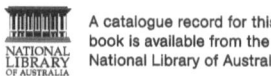 A catalogue record for this book is available from the National Library of Australia

ISBN: 9781763800991 (paperback)

This book is provided for informational purposes only and is not intended as a substitute for psychological, financial, legal or professional advice. The intent of the author is only to offer information of a general nature to help you in your quest for emotional, physical and spiritual wellbeing, however, individual circumstances vary. Readers should seek guidance from appropriately qualified professionals where necessary. In the event you use any of the information in this book for yourself, neither the publisher nor the author accepts any liability for any loss, damage or disruption arising from reliance on the information contained in this book. This includes but is not limited to direct, indirect, incidental, special or consequential damages. By engaging with this material, readers acknowledge personal responsibility for their own choices and actions.

The Kind Press acknowledges the Traditional Owners of Country throughout Australia and acknowledges their continuing connection to land, waters and community. We pay our respects to the people, the cultures and the Elders past and present.

*To the men whose love has shaped and moulded me into
becoming the woman I am today.
You were my love journey to
becoming my full self and who I was meant to be.*

Contents

Introduction ... 1

Part One: Okay, So Now You're Single, Where to Next

1. One of You Will Be This Person and One of You Will Be That One ... 7
2. Women Leave in Their Head First, Men With Their Feet ... 11
3. Sometimes Letting Go of the Dream Is Harder Than Letting Go of the Actual Person ... 12
4. Don't Sit Yourself Out, Please ... 14
5. You Divorced the Same Person You Married, They Didn't Change, You Did ... 15
6. Do You Want to Be Saved, or Do You Want to Be Fulfilled ... 19
7. You Are Going to Learn on People and People Are Going to Learn on You ... 22
8. Soulmates and Wound Mates, Which One Were You ... 25
9. My Marriage Ended but Theirs Didn't ... 29
10. First, Let Me Tell You Where You're Really Going ... 31
11. The Bridge of Space and Time Between Relationships ... 35
12. Spending Time on Your Own Without Someone in Your Bed or in Your Head ... 37
13. Our Queen Life Path, What Is It ... 40

14	Why Do We Avoid Fully Owning and Living Our Queen Life Path	44
15	Women Set the Tone	47
16	Life Is a Process of Levelling Up	48
17	For Those Who Suffered Emotional Abuse	49
18	What to Expect When You Go and Change the Boundaries on Your Ex	50
19	Self-Reflection Is Often an Arse, but We Can't Avoid It	52
20	The Thought of Being Naked With Someone Else	56
21	It Takes Two to Be Toxic	58
22	I Don't Want to Be Saved By a Man, but Where Do I Start Saving Myself	59
23	I Was Celibate for Twelve Months and This Is What I Learnt	62
24	My Money Story	64
25	Love Is Rare, Money Is Everywhere	70
26	You're Either a Woman With a $3,000 Handbag or a Woman With a $200 Handbag and $2,800 in the Bank	72
27	Whatever You Do Next, Make Sure It Brings You Fun	74
28	We Don't Manifest the End Result, We Manifest Everything in Between	75
29	Tell Me What You Want, What You Really, Really Want	77
30	Balancing Our Feminine and Masculine Energies to Attract Love and True Happiness	79
31	A Woman Only Has Room for One King in Her Heart	85
32	How to Drop Into and Embrace Our Feminine Energy	88
33	Everything Magic That Will Happen to You Will of Its Own Magic	94
34	Choosing From Your Worth Over Choosing From Your Wounds	97
35	When I Let People Love Me, They	99
36	How to Know What You Are Vibrationally Aligned for	101
37	Women, Stop Your Hunting, You're Not Good at It	102
38	Just Not That Into You, Why Low-Effort Men Trigger a Try Harder Response	104
39	Future Tripping and How We Sometimes Create Our Own Pain	107
40	Be Patient, Miracles Take Longer Than Settling Does	108

Part Two: The Queen Path. Moving on in Love After a Divorce

41	There Are No Wrong Partners	111
42	Why Are So Many Jaded About Love and Marriage	113
43	What Happily Married Couples Tell Me	115
44	What I Think About Many Marriages	116
45	Why Are We Seeing More Divorces Now Than Ever	119
46	I Want You to Start Seeing This Perspective	126
47	What Does It Really Mean When We Leave a Marriage	128
48	A Love Note to Men and Women Before We Go Any Further Together	131
49	What We Need to Understand About Ourselves as Humans	135
50	Why Finding Love After Divorce Is a Different Kind of Love Journey	138
51	Is the Grass Actually Greener	141
52	Love After Divorce and Love Within a Marriage	144
53	Life Paths and Soul Journeys	146
54	There Are Attractive People Everywhere but Soul Connections Are Rare	150
55	One Last Thing in Case You Feel Guilt About Divorce and Its Effect on Your Children	151
56	What Does a Next-Level Relationship Look Like	154
57	What Do We Desire From Love	156
58	Soulmate Love: The Person Family and Society Conditioned Us to Bring Home	158
59	Karmic Love: The Loves That Teach Us the Lessons We Don't Want to Have	162
60	The One Before the One: the Love That We Want to Work, That Shatters Our Soul When It Doesn't	166
61	Twin Flame Love: The Love That Makes Us Stop	168
62	Twin Flame Love: Real or Bullshit	172
63	Are Twin Flames Toxic	173

64	How to Know If Someone Is Your Twin Flame	174
65	The Stages Present Within a Twin Flame Connection	176
66	The Creation of Power Couples	178
67	Shifting From a Human, Ego-Led Life to a Soul-Led Life	180
68	Choosing to Ignore the Soul Journey Within	183
69	Grief and Letting Go to Move on	185
70	Trusting the Timeline of Your Love Journey	187
71	Fearing You Will End Up Alone and Never Find Love	189
72	Staying Above the Car Crash That Can Be the Dating Pool	191
73	Coming to Love From a Place of Fix Me, Save Me or Make Me Feel Better About Myself	192
74	Holding Onto Someone Believing They're Your One	194
75	Attached More Than You Are in Love	196
76	Expressing Your Needs and Truth	197
77	Over-Focusing on Love and Finding a Partner	198
78	Embracing the Season You're in	200
79	Overcoming Your Childhood and Its Imprint on Your Psyche	203
80	When You Keep Attracting a Type	207
81	Putting Your Desire for a Connection With Someone Else Above Your Love for Self	209
82	Letting Go of a Love That Has Come to an End in Your Life	210
83	Managing Manipulative Exes Who Continue to Trigger You and Impact Your Life	212
84	Situationships and Non-Committal Lovers: What to Do With Them	216
85	Affairs and Third-Party Situations	218
86	Attaching to New Love Fast	221
87	When Your Heart Has Been Broken Too Many Times	223
88	Fearing Vulnerability	225
89	Ignoring Your Intuition to Stay in a Relationship	226
90	Becoming an Energetic Match for Your Ideal Partner	228
91	For Those Who Are More Comfortable Giving Love Than Receiving It	230

92	People-Pleasing and the Desire to Please	232
93	We All Deserve Love but Some of Us Are Less Ready Than We Realise	234
94	Leading With Appearances	235
95	Applying Rules of Right and Wrong to Love	237
96	Understanding the Feminine and Masculine in Love	238
97	Feeling Disheartened While on the Love Journey	242
98	A Bird's-Eye View of You: What Is Your Current Life Path Hurdle	244
99	The Tao: Finding Your Own Inner Balance and Path to Your Alignment	245
100	Bringing to Life Your Best Scenario and Not Your Worst	247
101	What Does This Person Bring Out in Me, the Best and the Worst	248
102	If I Let Go of My Attachment, What Is Love Teaching Me	249
103	What Was It About Them That Made Me Love Being Around	250

Acknowledgements	255

Introduction

Many people approach ending their marriage and getting a divorce much like many parents approach having a first child. They become so consumed in the birth plan, setting up the nursery, the baby shower, understanding the in-utero growth, that they give little thought or planning to the biggest journey of all: raising a child for the next 18 years and beyond. I know it was true for me when I was deep in my own thoughts about my marriage in 2014 and 2015, before I finally found the confidence to say the words out loud.

It's something I hear reflected in my clients' experiences too. The inner turmoil that comes with coming to a decision confidently enough so that we can own it resolutely enough as our truth to express the words out loud. It leaves no head space or emotional bandwidth in that moment to allow a person to even begin to process or turn their gaze to the biggest journey of all.

The future.
The road ahead.
The next season of life.
The next chapter of who we are becoming.

With hindsight, I can tell you, from the perspective of someone many years beyond the end of her marriage, that you will look back and realise the leaving was the easiest part. The real journey is finding yourself, especially if you never truly knew who you were as a woman.

Discovering who you are, creating a life you love, and, if it calls to you, finding love again, that is the journey. The end of your marriage, much like giving birth, becomes a single moment in the entire story. Your ex, your relationship, and even who you were during that time become distant memories of a past version of yourself. For me, it has been a nine-year journey of growth to become the woman I am today. Someone very different from who I once imagined myself to be, living a life I never expected. And yet, I wouldn't change a thing. I'd like to suggest the possibility that this might be true for you too.

If you are leaving your marriage without a strong sense of who you are, like I did, you may not yet be able to see your fullest potential or all that you can become in the future. What you believe you want, who you think you are, and the sort of love partner that is a true love match for you, will change as you step deeper and deeper onto the path of finding yourself and becoming yourself.

Finding a true love match, whether that is a high-quality soulmate or a twin flame, becomes the cherry on top to the journey of becoming you. And after experiencing the energetic imprint of all three types of love unions in my personal life: the soulmate, the karmic and the twin flame, what I know to be true is this. The love journey grows you by breaking you first.

There are some wounds that can only come to light in relationships, especially karmic ones. In fact, karmic relationships are often where the deepest healing happens! And that is the journey. It is an unavoidable one that we must walk to find true love in our life that lasts. A love where someone is stuck on you, not stuck with you. A very different love path than the one we walked to become married. A very different love path we danced to stay married by self-abandoning, ignoring our intuition, people pleasing, staying married for validation or out of fear that we might end up alone or unable to financially thrive. Insert your favourite fear or flavour here that is unique to you.

I left my marriage in 2016 as a stay-at-home mum. At the time, my now-thriving coaching business was just a side hustle. I was 34. My daughters were four and five. I had never had a bill in my own name or financially provided for myself. I hadn't been with another man since I was 21. I had no idea who I was, and only the tiniest of sense within of who I felt I could be, who I was meant to be. That tiniest of sense within has been what I have chased and what has guided me forward since.

Today, as I write this in 2025, I am a successful entrepreneur and businesswoman with a self-made, multiple six-figure business. My daughters, now 13 and 14, live primarily with their dad, while I have relocated to the other side of the country, called there to fulfil my mission and to live in the place where I was meant to be.

I am working with a shaman in Dubai on topics that would blow your mind, and it continues to blow my mind that this is my life path and meant for me. I have coached thousands of men and women, supporting them to leave and move on from their marriage having ended. I have guided clients to set up and grow businesses, advance their careers, make life-altering decisions, and navigate the love journey to find true connection.

I can do this for them because I have done it for myself first. I am wiser, more spiritual, more feminine, smarter, and more deeply connected to myself than I ever imagined I would be. What was once the tiniest sense of within has come to life over the years in ways I could never have predicted. In meant-to-be ways I could never have shaped or made happen other than the way they did.

This is the book my 2016 self would have desperately wanted to read. It would have helped her make sense of what she was experiencing, given her reassurance, and brought her peace. I hope it does for you. My sincerest wishes and hope is that my journey and words inside this book guide and inspire you forward on your path.

With love,
Carla Da Costa
xox

Part One

Okay, So Now You're Single, Where to Next

1
ONE OF YOU WILL BE THIS PERSON AND ONE OF YOU WILL BE THAT ONE

When a relationship ends, I see this pattern occur almost every instance. Both of you will move on in your own time. However, one of you will stay very much the same person and the other will change, grow and evolve into a completely different version of themselves, without meaning to. If we reflect on this, the phenomenon makes sense. Because a healthy, fulfilling relationship ideally consists of two people continually growing and evolving into themselves individually. Choosing to return together in love, alongside one another through it all. When one of us stops, when one of us begins to contract or pull back emotionally, physically or intimately, things will always start to brew. And none of it is usually positive.

Stagnancy. The intimacy dies. Resentment. Boredom. Loss of passion. Disconnection. If this dynamic hadn't existed, the marriage would have continued into a happily-ever-after story. Two evolving and open-hearted individuals moving and loving one another alongside their life journey.

So, what do I know to be true here? The person who stays very much the same will move on quickly in their new life. Maybe through their life or professional experience, during the marriage they were already living their life path or the one they wish to live. They are already living at their fullest self-expression. The only thing they need is a partner who is a supportive match to their existing desires and path. They are happily content in their own skin and life, regardless of your feelings or thoughts about it.

Often a woman's self-growth does take a back seat in a relationship because she has had children. This is usually the equation here as the role often falls to the woman. And someone needed to earn money and strive in their career. This role often falls to the man. The person who will stay very much the same will most likely go on to choose a new partner for themselves quickly. They will avoid being on their own and choose to jump straight into a new relationship as soon as they can, literally replacing their ex with someone else. Perhaps with someone similar to their ex. They know what they want and who they are. And they will choose a partner and life that supports them to stay this version of themselves. They will look like a success post-divorce. Moving on beautifully. Kudos to this person. If you're on a winning formula, you know who you are and you're not hurting anyone, then stick with what's working for you.

Whether this is you or not, know this about this person. The same personal and relationship issues that caused their relationship to break down and end before, will follow them into their next relationship, if they are not explored and resolved. Life is a series of lessons and what we choose to not see in ourselves only ever presents itself to us later. The same lesson, just dressed up in different clothes. The universe is brilliant like that! Until we learn it, the lesson will continue to present itself to us.

I once said to my ex-husband's girlfriend when she made a complaint about him to me, 'I don't know what to say. He's the same guy I met when I was twenty-one, only now he's older, drives a better car and has a bigger house.' While this might not be entirely true, also it kind of is. So, if you're not the one staying the same, this makes you the grower out of the two of you.

Hello, kindred, aligned and growing soul! In life, we can only avoid the growth we need to do for so long before the universe makes us so uncomfortable that we can no longer ignore it. I see you. You're changing life paths. Upgrading your inner hardware. Ascending higher to a life and lifestyle that feels more aligned with who you really are. Levelling up your soul system within. Who even were you? Did you know who you were before? Who the hell are you now? I liken this process of changing life paths and upgrading our inner hardware to finally skipping the scratch on a record we've been stuck on going over and over. It's a literal picking up of the needle and placing it forward onto the next song. We always knew deep down that there was a next song to enjoy. We always felt a silent desire and pull to explore it and move on.

Welcome to your own personal growth journey, where you will look back on yourself today and wonder how you were ever married to that guy for as long as you were and how you tolerated it. You at your absolute best. This is going to be more than just about finding a new partner for yourself. Sorry to tell you this if you thought this was the journey. This is you choosing life and love from your worth and not from your wound. The call to stay the same is tempting, I won't deny. It's a warm bath of familiarity and comfort. I never judge anyone else's journey or what they choose to do. Neither should you. Each to their own divine journey.

Change is often uncomfortable, but the result is always stunning and beautiful. Cue image of a butterfly slowly emerging from its cocoon. If you have unwittingly found yourself on the path of growth and change, embrace it. It's where you need to be, and your life will forever be changed by what you embrace and move through in this space of time.

While your ex who stayed the same might outwardly look like a success post-divorce, ticking all the boxes relationship-wise, career-wise and financially, you perhaps, for a little while, outwardly might not. Your journey might look a little slower, your wins might look small or non-existent to others. But know that your life will carry you to where you need to be, at the right time for you, and it will be even better than you can imagine now.

It always does. Trust me.

2
WOMEN LEAVE IN THEIR HEAD FIRST, MEN WITH THEIR FEET

A woman is often done in her head long before she leaves with her feet. This is almost always true. There's a certain line that a woman crosses in her head of 'I'm done'. Once crossed, there's really no calling her back over it. She's gone.

She might stay for the kids, for financial reasons, but in her head, she's making love to someone else, anyone to make her feel like a passionate, appreciated woman again. This was certainly my journey. And if you're the one who chose to leave your marriage, it is probably yours. I expressed my emotions. Felt unheard and shut down. I closed myself emotionally and then I shut down physically on my marriage. I closed up sexual shop for twelve months and I weighed up my guilt, wondered whether our relationship could actually ever improve for the long term, considered my future if I were to leave and sat with its possible impact before I finally decided to leave. I won't touch on men here other than to say that biologically they are wired differently, and we should never compare ourselves.

I want to gift you the freedom and the release to know it's not just you moving through a relationship ending in this way. It is almost everyone. After years of working with women in this season of their life, believe me when I tell you that this is very much true.

3
SOMETIMES LETTING GO OF THE DREAM IS HARDER THAN LETTING GO OF THE ACTUAL PERSON

I left my marriage of my own choosing, but by no means did I leave it high-fiving the world and kicking up my heels with glee. I left my marriage carrying a lot of hurt, disappointment and sadness. At what it had been and what it could have been. At this time in my life, newly divorced and acting like I didn't care, underneath I still did. I was carrying a deep sense of loss at the potential I'd seen in our future together and sadness at the now gaping chasm between what I'd always hoped would be my story and what I could now see was the reality.

A marriage ending is a grieving process and, depending on how it ended, you either grieved for its loss while you were married, or you will grieve for its loss after it ended. Or like me, both. Either way, there is a grieving, and often it is always more about the loss of the dream than it is the loss of the actual person.

Grief comes and goes in waves, whatever the death might be, a person passing away, a dream ending, the loss feels the same. Grief is not a straight line. When you think you are over it, life shows you a memory and you realise you are still quite not. Walking away from a marriage, whether by choice or consequence, moves very much in the same way. Just when you think you're good, your ex will move on or move to another suburb, or your children will go from living at yours most of the time to living at their dads just as much.

There is always a new something to adjust to, until one day there is not. I'm not sure if grief really ever goes away, or if grief one day just turns itself into gratitude and beautiful memories without you realising it has transformed itself. I think it's more we just learn to live without something we once thought we couldn't. But know, grief always does become easier to live with if we let go and allow it to pass.

4
DON'T SIT YOURSELF OUT, PLEASE

I hear many women say they're done with love. A lot of women think and feel this way at different parts of their journey out of love and a marriage. Men do too, of course. It's easy to leave a marriage and to feel jaded about love. I've heard it all. 'I'll never get married again.' 'I'll never live with someone again.' 'I couldn't take being hurt again like this.' 'I'd rather be on my own.' When I hear these things what I know I'm really hearing is 'I'm hurting.' And what I know is really going on is that they haven't stopped hurting enough to meet the right person for themselves yet. That person who will sweep in out of nowhere and change everything for them, cracking their heart wide open again in the process. That person who finds love again is actually the majority. The person who chooses to stay on their own, or ends up on their own, forever hiding from love, is the minority.

You might not see this now, but I do. Please, don't sit yourself out. You're hurt now. This doesn't mean you will be hurt forever. Let yourself feel however you do. And know you won't be in this space forever.

5
YOU DIVORCED THE SAME PERSON YOU MARRIED, THEY DIDN'T CHANGE, YOU DID

I have a handful of life moments where truth brought me to my knees. Myself, lying naked on the floor of a beautiful rainfall-style shower at a hotel, post moving out of the marital home, was one of my more profound. In that moment, all the pain that my past choices had caused me literally had me floored. The pain of my mistakes was so overwhelming it became immobilising. I'd never felt more abandoned and let down by those around me. And I'd never felt more abandoned by my own self.

I had spent my adult life mostly putting everyone's needs and intentions for me above my own. In a way living someone else's life path. Playing a supportive role in my husband's life with no real thought to my own because he had been the stronger personality with the bigger, more ambitious goals. Now I was paying the price. In that shower moment, I realised that where I found myself shouldn't be coming as a surprise. Self-abandonment is a thing. Almost a bigger thing than when others abandon us. It cut deeply to acknowledge to myself all the times I'd dismissed my intuition and acted against it, ignored and downplayed my feelings. Let myself be shut down, silenced or pretended I didn't need in my life what I did, connection, affection, intimacy, kindness, understanding. You can tolerate so many things for the sake of a marriage until one day you can't.

I changed the rules on my ex-husband when I asked for a separation and divorce. He was content with how things were. They suited him. He might not have been happy, but he was okay and for him that was enough. And of course, our marriage was going to feel okay for him. I'd enabled him to be the way he was and to stay that way for as long as he had. It was me who changed the rules. Me who changed, me who said, 'I'm done.'

So, when it came to the week of packing up and moving out of the marital home, rather than the support I had been expecting, because I saw our marriage failing as a reflection of us both, I received a 'you wanted the divorce, so you can do the packing up' response. And he took his new girlfriend away for a holiday and left me with our daughters both under the age of four, to pack up an entire house and move out. Thank God for good friends who helped me pack. Thank God for good friends who picked me up off the hotel shower floor. Thank God for the boyfriend who I'd been seeing who chose to break up with me in the middle of it all. He too was going through a divorce and couldn't be there for me during my own. We always meet our mirrors, including during those times.

There are many beautiful, amazing things that come with being resilient. We can withstand much of what life throws at us with strength and grace. But it also means that it takes a tonne of shit to crack us open to face our pain and shadow, as we all need to at times in our life. I could have withstood the solo move physically and emotionally. I'm robust like that. I was coping and mostly good ... right up until the boyfriend, who I hoped was going to save me from the mess but broke up with me. I am also forever grateful for him behaving like he did and for the complete cracking open I needed. I was a thirty-something woman leaving a marriage that her twenty-one-year-old self willingly chose. Pursued even.

My ex-husband softened slightly during our twelve years together, but he didn't change all that much. I did. All the things I'd kept silent, I could no longer ignore. All the things I'd pretended weren't important to me, I could no longer deny. All the things I'd repressed, ignored and glossed over were now just sitting, glaring at my soul, asking me to acknowledge them. And my ex-boyfriend, he hadn't changed either. He'd always been too focused on himself and his own pain to ever really be able to support me through mine. I'd willing chosen both of these men and handed myself over to be loved by them. If I'm honest with myself, I'd chosen my own pain and heartache. I was walking away from the same men I'd originally said yes to.

I cursed my twenty-one-year-old self for wanting and needing so much to be chosen by someone else, for needing to be in a relationship because it made her feel validated and enough and for doing this to the point of abandoning her own self and needs. I cursed my divorced self for believing a man so wrapped up in his own separation pain could possibly change enough to be there for mine. For putting energy into saving him, over putting that energy into saving myself.

The lesson I've learnt is that we should never be down on our younger selves for the decisions and choices they made. I do believe everything happens for the right reason; every step leads us to the next wonderful one. Whether you were twenty-one or thirty-five, you made the best decision you could then with everything that you knew about love and life. All you knew about love, relationships and self-worth had been modelled to you by your parents or caregivers, rightly or wrongly. And while maybe you were choosing a relationship more from your wounds over your worth, beautifully, so was your ex-partner.

Two souls, moving through life and trying to do their best. How can you be angry with yourself for that. How can you be angry with them for that either. What a divine and loving lesson of forgiveness of self and others to reflect on. To realise and acknowledge, with the passage of time, how much more you know and see now. And whether your ex is able to share the same perception or not, no matter. It can still be yours.

6
DO YOU WANT TO BE SAVED, OR DO YOU WANT TO BE FULFILLED

I was the girl looking to be saved when I left my marriage. I didn't see it at the time, but I do now.

Dear future man,
Save me from not feeling good enough because I'm on my own.
Save me from having to find myself.
Save me from my aloneness.
Save me from learning to stand on my two financially independent feet as a woman.
Save me from having to make hard decisions on my own.
Save me from having to work on myself.
Save me, please.

Three weeks after my ex-husband moved out of our family home, I locked eyes with a handsome guy on the dance floor of a pub. He caught my attention straight away. I was newly out of what felt like a loveless marriage, and I can see that the reason I became attached to this *particular* guy so fast was because he made me feel sexy, appreciated and seen after feeling so numb. It was enticing after feeling nothing for so long. I wanted it to be love, and in all honesty, I assumed he was going to be my next long-term relationship and forever guy. I was so well-conditioned to being in a long-term relationship that it never crossed my mind it would be a short-term one. Or that maybe all I needed was for it to be a short-term one. This didn't end so well for me. So, how are we going to spend this time between partners and our next life paths?

People who avoid saving themselves and look for someone else to save them (like I was), often attract and pursue one of two types of people into their life. Because women are empathetic and nurturing souls, we easily attract men into our lives who need saving too. They become the project to work on instead of ourselves. A project that beautifully distracts us from our own self-work. Or we attract someone who swoops in, saves us and solves all of our problems. Reads like perfection, but ultimately, we have given our power over from the start in this relationship dynamic. We look to him for our answers and our life path, we give him that role, and ultimately, he will thrive on it. Sometimes to the point of controlling.

My time spent lying naked on the shower floor of the hotel was when I realised, I'd looked to every man in my past to save me in some way. I'd given the keys to my life and self-worth over to my husband as a twenty-one-year-old, only to find my thirty-something self feeling suffocated, stifled and controlled by it all. And I'd fallen into the arms of my newest boyfriend hoping he'd save me from myself and my situation. Only to discover he needed saving himself. Stuff you both. I'd love to tell you that I sat up from the shower floor in a space of newly found enlightenment after being dumped. I did not. I sat up in complete, utter pain. And I continued needing to be saved. Sometimes seeking out others to save me within the space of a relationship. Other times, I muddied through the self-work on my own.

Until one day, I did not. I was saving myself. In fact, I had saved myself. And I began looking for someone who'd saved themselves too. A person who needs saving and avoids saving themselves generally goes on to inadvertently do one of two things to us in a relationship. Thanks to your love and support, they grow their own wings and fly away on you. You've saved them, healed them and they don't need your saving energy anymore. Or they will continue to always need you to save them. I've played both of those roles in love and life. And neither felt good. I don't recommend them.

Which leads me to my next point.

7
YOU ARE GOING TO LEARN ON PEOPLE AND PEOPLE ARE GOING TO LEARN ON YOU

You are going to hurt people as you move through this period of your life, intentionally or not. And people are going to hurt you as they move through this period of their life, intentionally or not. Sorry to inform you of this. This is life, not just after divorce. This is life, at any time. People will always learn more about themselves through their relationships with others than they do on their own.

Let's be honest with ourselves here. It's easy to perceive ourselves as having it together when there's no one reflecting back to us that we do not. The wiser and more attentive we are, realising that everyone is learning on one another, the better, more compassionate beings we are. And this is true in life and relationships in general. This doesn't mean there will be a cascade of heartbreak coming for you in your future, just that this is how humans move through life, in both their energy of kindness and of malice. There are more good people in the world than there are bad. There are more well-intentioned people than there are narcissistic and self-serving. Always remember that.

Every human is simply moving through life, seeking to have their needs met in some way. Their needs for love, connection, financial security, success. For fun, fresh air, significance, purpose. When we start taking more of a living-above-the-matrix view on life, over being caught in the middle of it, you will observe men, women and children doing just this. I need to feel loved. How can I feel this, in this moment? I need to feel peace. How can I create this? I need to feel fit and alive in my body. What will I do today to feel more like this? We learn and unlearn on others throughout our entire life. It's best to look at most adults who were hardwired as children to move through life, trying to get their needs met in the best way possible. Parents showed us what love looked like and how to behave so we could continue to receive love from them. And as adults, we seek out and recreate the same energy and feel of what we were modelled. Or in some instances, where our childhood was somewhat negative, we deliberately choose something different for ourselves. Any relationship that we choose early on in life is most likely going to be based on our conditioning. One chosen much less from a point of adult awareness—which makes sense, because in our twenties and thirties we are in many ways still growing into adults. What does this mean? We chose someone to marry not really understanding why we chose them.

They made us feel good. They chose us, which made us feel good enough. Desired what we desired. We shared similar values, interests or life goals. Our social circles overlapped, or our backgrounds aligned in ways that felt familiar. It made sense, looked and felt sensible and was likely met with approval from those around us. But none of this considers what's really going on underneath. The relating styles that both bring to the relationship. The attachment styles we arrived with that we learnt from our parents. The unrealised traumas and the beliefs, both positive and negative, that exist due to our upbringing. We all carry these patterns and dynamics, whether we are aware of it or not, into our first marriage, and as a consequence the relationship often bears the brunt of much of them being played out in a cycle.

I brought their behaviours, expectations and fears into my first marriage despite them being amazing parents. And my ex-husband brought his. When I look back at the undoings of our marriage, our dynamic as a couple as we bounced off one another during our thirteen years, everything that we brought out in one another without meaning to, the good and the bad. None of it now comes as a surprise. We are not to blame for this phenomenon. This is life. Some couples genuinely move through their own unlearnings together and emerge a better, more connected couple for doing so. The love grows, intimacy deepens. But for many couples. Their relationship was left carrying the cost and burden of unlearning, accidentally on each other with other dynamics: resentment, loss of trust, lack of sex or sex being used as a tool to manipulate, emotional shutdowns, a lack of honesty, words being left unsaid and financial manipulation.

I used to envy couples in their forties and fifties after my divorce. Their families, their deep history, finances and everything they built as a couple still together. But now, I don't. After years of working with many people who feel stuck in these relationships, I see too many falsities and self-compromises in so many of them. It's not because I don't believe in marriage or long-term relationships. It's not because I don't believe they're possible. I deeply do. Only now I believe in only being in the right one. In relationships that genuinely light up my inner and outer world.

Most of us will move through a number of wound mate style relationships before we evolve into a space where we are open and ready for more of a deeper connected love. I've learnt that the most poignant question in our journey into our next love is: how soulmate ready am I really? Ready enough that I am able to consciously stop cycling myself through versions of the same wound mate relationship—different guy, treating me in a similar or the same way, with the same result. Consciously choosing to not go there. Because what I do know is this. We will continue to attract a similar shade of the same person until we've done the loving work on ourselves. Truth.

8
SOULMATES AND WOUND MATES, WHICH ONE WERE YOU

Soulmates are rare, but it's not because they don't exist. It's because we are only just beginning to feel culturally able to release relationships and marriages that no longer serve us. An undoing process that ultimately opens us up to entering our next level of partnership, evolving with us as we evolve upwards in ourselves. Can you see the beauty in this? This ability to ascend higher in love by detaching from the idea that it must be our first love who must be the person for us. Can you see that the only thing stopping it from unfolding beautifully of its own accord, that keeps us stuck in our wound cycle, is our perception and fear of how long the process might take to find that love. Fears that we might end up alone, unloved or financially struggling? (Whichever fear it might be for you.)

Many of us chose a wound mate style relationship first or even several times over without realising. Often cycling through many wound mate relationships, encountering shades of the same people and results, until we eventually (hopefully!) evolved ourselves forward. So, which one were you, wound mates, or soulmates?

Wound mates
- Relationship feels like it's on a cycle of drama and the same issues repeat themselves and never fully resolve.
- Connection based on unresolved trauma, low self-worth, low self-belief. The relationship validates your need to look and feel good enough.
- You seek to fix or save each other.

- Feels intoxicating, chaotic, addictive and unpredictable. Push/pull energy.
- Reflects unhealthy dynamics with parents and childhood experience.

Soulmates
- Relationship feels healing. You feel seen, heard and appreciated for being you.
- Shared values, outlook on life, vitality. The connection supports you growing together as individuals and as a couple.
- You empower each other.
- Feels grounded and consistent, and flows.
- Relationship has been consciously created and comes together as a result of each individual's growth. The relationship is not a reflection of your parents' dynamic nor a deliberate attempt to be in something different from your parents' dynamic. It just is.

I was not an energetic match for a soulmate relationship in my twenties. I wouldn't have attracted one nor pursued one. I was not ready for such a love. The flow and calm would not have felt attractive or push/pull enough. I couldn't have possibly held such a thing because I didn't have the emotional awareness. I would have wasted such a love. I was not ready for it. I had not evolved in myself enough. My journey is true for many. Learning on others and others learning on us is our collective spirit evolving at our own loving, upward pace toward a relationship that is closer to that of a soulmate. Can you see how different this journey is going to be for everyone in its pace and in its lessons? Depending on our conditioning and past experience, some of us have a little to learn and some of us have a lot. And that's okay.

I want you to know many people are recovering after leaving a wound mate style relationship. So many. I want you to know many people are stuck in wound mate style relationships and fear leaving. So many. By definition, a soulmate relationship is this: two souls coming together who have done or are doing the inner work on themselves. Neither is a perfectly evolved version of themselves (no one is that), but they have evolved out of their desire and need to be saved, to be living in a cycle of trauma, drama and arguing about the same things. And they are no longer addicted to the energetic push/pull nature that wounded relationships bring. Instead, someone who seeks or is ready to be in a soulmate relationship desires flow, calmness, intimacy, affection and shared growth, and is comfortable with being fully seen. The connection is everything to this person. They don't need to be saved, and they don't want to save anyone either. They come together with one another, and they just are.

I've seen this in my personal life and I'm not going to lie, putting words on this feeling is hard. But when you know, you know. The difference between a wounded relationship and a soulmate relationship is in the foundation that you bring to one another. Energy doesn't lie, here.

So, if we consider what it is that makes a soulmate relationship, two individuals doing the inner work on themselves, then our role in the journey becomes this: to be a soul who is doing the inner work on themselves. How can we expect from another what we are not truly doing ourselves? The universe won't deliver on that. A soulmate-ready man will find you attractive because of your evolved nature too. He is not going to seek out a relationship with a woman who still hasn't found at her core her own stability and sense of self, who is still needing to be saved. Who still seeks constant validation because of her anxiety, wounds and trust issues.

No one seeks perfection. No one has fully evolved. But if you seek the peace, love and commitment of a soulmate relationship, we first need to be an energetic match for one. We need to evolve into a woman who can hold such a love without fear of it being too good to be true or of it leaving her. Whether someone is ready or wants to do the work on themselves is their journey. We can only ever control ours. And ultimately, if someone chooses not to do the work on themselves, in my eyes, this is evidence that the relationship is a wound mate relationship, not a soulmate relationship—regardless of its potential.

Do the work on yourself, beautiful; stay firmly on your life path and move forward with that energy. The right people for you will find you on your journey too. Seek ease, fun and growth, whether or not those around you seek it for themselves. It's yours to have. Yes, some people will fall away in the journey, but they are always, ALWAYS, replaced by others more aligned with our truth once we're standing in it.

9
MY MARRIAGE ENDED BUT THEIRS DIDN'T

Once seen, we can't unsee this wound mate knowledge. It will change your perception of relationships in your life forever. The ones you have had, the ones you are in and the ones around you. At least, it did for me. You will spot wound mates around you now, doing their best because they genuinely want the best for themselves and for their families. Some will be functioning better than others or at least presenting that they are.

Healers will tell you that the more soulmates that come together in this world, the higher the level of consciousness it will bring collectively to those around us. An energetic shift from woundedness to love on a collective, generational scale. How divine.

The most beautiful example here is to ask ourselves and imagine: Who would I be if my parents had been soulmate lovers? How different would my choices in love be? And if we were to take it another generation onwards: If I were that person and love had been demonstrated to me in that way as the standard, I should expect for myself, then who would that make my children today, having watched me love in that energy?

People accept, tolerate and excuse many behaviours in the name of love. Or at least to stay in a relationship over not being in one. (Please note in no way am I including situations of domestic violence or fear for personal safety in this statement.) The truth is that not everyone desires a soulmate. They just want a mate over not having one.

This is going to be why some of your friends and family who are in wound mate style relationships will potentially struggle to understand your choice to leave your marriage. They might have opinions. And they'll vicariously live through you, watching to see how you go as a measure of how they might if they were to leave their marriage. Or they'll project onto you their own fears and beliefs, my favourites being, 'I'd hate to be out there dating now' and 'the grass isn't always greener'. Ultimately, these are all their beliefs and fears. Beliefs and fears that are holding them back from moving forward in their own lives. They don't have to be yours.

A lot of people in your life are going to stay in their wound mate relationships. They will adjust their expectations and behaviour to live with and manage their situation. The truth for us, though, is once we've said goodbye to that wounded cycle, it's very hard to go back into one with our eyes closed. In all my years coaching clients I've never had someone leave a wound mate relationship and look back on it with regret for having left. Their only regret, if they do have one, is that they didn't leave sooner. Most of our relationships are meant to teach us lessons, not to actually last forever. Not every love is supposed to last. Feel the freedom over the fear in this. The truth is, we accept relationships that mirror how we feel about ourselves, and we let go of relationships when our soul and spirit can no longer stay quiet and acknowledge we deserve and desire more. And that journey, that line in concrete of *I deserve more, and I can't go back,* is going to look different for everyone.

10
FIRST, LET ME TELL YOU WHERE YOU'RE REALLY GOING

Sometimes there's what we think we need and want and then there's what we actually need and want. Just for a little moment, I'd love for you to remove from the table any desire for love to come along and sweep you off your feet. At least while you're reading this chapter! If you left a relationship that felt loveless for a long time, then I completely understand your desire to find love, passion and attention. If sex, intimacy and connection is something you haven't felt in a long time, then this might be something you need to experience again however it looks or feels. Whether it's 'forever' for you or not. It doesn't matter. And that's called being human. I would also love for you to consider what this season of your life is really going to be about for you. What it needs to be about for you when you're ready.

So often we hand over our sense of self and trade in our identity as a woman when we marry and welcome motherhood. We don't mean to. It comes with the wife and mum territory. To identify with both means we were invested in those areas of our life, which is beautiful. But it's also why women so easily can lose themselves. I loved being a wife and a mother. Enjoyed sharing and setting up a home for us all. And I loved being a stay-at-home mum. I was so blessed that I was able to be that for the first years of my daughters' lives before they started school. You never get that time back as a mum. I did all the things. Made Pinterest boards of home interiors and design. Tried out new recipes. Home cooked for my daughters as much as possible and tried to create an environment that was healthy, supportive and loving for them. iPad time, but not too much.

Park and beach hangs with friends and their kids. Babycino dates. All the things. I really threw myself into the role of mum and it was a wonderful, blissed-up time in my life.

Then I became the soccer mum and Uber mum. My time started to facilitate my kid's lives more than it did my own in many ways. But I did it happily, knowing I was creating for them a beautiful, big life of friendships, interests and self-confidence. The price of this, though, is that we can lose our sense of ourselves as women, separate from being a wife, a mother and everything else to everyone else. Everything becomes about others first. Women are so easily selfless in this season of life. Men can be too.

Going through a separation and divorce truly moves you into a new season of being a woman, whether you wish to be here or not. I believe women move through many seasons as we move through life. More than men do. Seasons that often completely change us to our core. Wife. Mother. Lover. Career Woman. Perimenopause. Menopause. Goddess Queen. Grandmother.

I love my daughters with all of my heart. I held on to having them for the majority of time after I left my marriage, for as long as my ex-husband and growing career allowed. They have always been my priority and continue to be. Now I find myself in a new season. And this is the point I'm leading you to… rediscovering you.

One of the biggest positives after a divorce (once you've emotionally adjusted to it) is the time you now have set aside for yourself that is child-free. Time that is now all yours, to do with as you please. In my marriage, I was the primary caregiver for our daughters. Getting time out and away from them took forward planning and negotiation. It felt like hard work to organise. So, for me, it rarely happened. But now, post-divorce, my time is delightfully my own. At first, I felt lost in all this free time away from my daughters. I didn't know what to do with myself, and I had very little to fill this time with, to be honest. It took time to create, but now my time is wonderfully full to the brim.

In hindsight, I don't believe women should lose themselves in their children to the point of self-sacrifice. I don't believe it's healthy. I write this fully acknowledging that this is how I moved through that particular season of my life and that I have very few regrets about it. But still, there is no gold star or prize for taking on that kind of role, only a loss of self that goes on to impact us and impact our relationships. Rediscovering who you are now as a woman is your journey. Not finding a man who is going to make it all shiny, happy and better. Sorry! I know that I didn't want to hear this when I was newly out of my divorce. I wanted the exact opposite. To walk straight into the loving arms of my next someone. And it did happen like that, as you know. What you value in a man and what sort of man you need in your life. All of it is going to look and feel different for you now in this season because you are a different woman.

Your journey and life will become yours as much as your children's will become theirs. The more you own yours, the more they will own theirs. I've watched my daughters blossom and grow through the osmosis of watching me as I have blossomed and grown. Every next step up that I take, they take it with me through observance. Now this is the new normal. Now this is the standard. This is how love looks, sounds and feels for Mum, which is how it will look, sound and feel for me. This is how it looks, sounds and feels for a woman who is stepping into her fullest self-expression and fun, which is how life will look, sound and feel for me. Can you see how it goes?

Stop living life through your children, if up until now you have been. Stop hiding behind them instead of rediscovering you. Start living life for you again. This doesn't make you selfish. This doesn't make you less of a mother. This makes you beautifully whole. Life after divorce is going to be less about finding love for you. It's going to be more about rediscovering you.

11
THE BRIDGE OF SPACE AND TIME BETWEEN RELATIONSHIPS

How you choose to spend time between relationships is going to define your next relationship. It will shape who you attract and who you choose to pursue and let in next. I see so many men and women jump back into the dating pool over and over again. The same person with the same fears of intimacy, of being fully seen for all shades of themselves. The same feelings of not being good enough. The same desire to not be alone, to feel validated. All hoping for a different result. This is like having the ingredients for a chocolate cake and hoping it's going to come out of the oven an apple cake because you stirred the batter anticlockwise this time instead of clockwise. The same ingredients will always give you the same results. Every time! Or I see women sitting out of the dating world almost entirely. They just don't have the heart or confidence to put themselves out there again and risk being hurt or disappointed, perhaps occasionally opening their online dating account to see what's out there on a lonely night at home.

Healing between relationships doesn't require a timeline of you must be single for this long or you must do this and that. Healing does require healing work, though. Time being single without doing some healing work to bring yourself closer to rediscovering you, the woman you are underneath all the layers of guardedness and hurt, is a little bit like lost time. It's hiding, not healing. And that's okay. But it won't bring you closer into alignment with yourself again so that you can understand why you attract and pursue what you do in love and life and change it. Why you've accepted and settled for breadcrumbs instead of owning your desire to have the whole cake and then some.

The healing is what's going to elevate you to the next level of attracting all that's amazing for you into your life. What you deserve. Not the tighter booty, not the fancy handbag, not the perfect nails, hair, wardrobe, house or bank account. None of that truly matters as much as we think it does.

12

SPENDING TIME ON YOUR OWN WITHOUT SOMEONE IN YOUR BED OR IN YOUR HEAD

Welcome to the dating pool, if you've dared to venture out there yet! There are souls at varying stages all jumping from one relationship and person to the next. All in an attempt to avoid themselves. Are you excited yet? Filled with people re-entering the dating pool for the first time in years, now different from who they were when they were last single, carrying new wounds and fears, much of it still unrealised, hoping for a happy result, whether short or long term. It's heartbreaking, in a way, to think about it like this. Grown adults, many of them fearful of being on their own, of ending up alone, seeking to be loved by another to fill the void that being on their own leaves them feeling. It's no wonder the modern dating pool can sometimes feel like a minefield.

Emotionally avoidant and unavailable people who aren't in a place to be fully invested jump straight into online dating unhealed after a break up. Perpetuating their avoidant cycle by never getting too close or intimate with someone. You can't get hurt again if you only ever keep your connections surface level, right? And anxious attachers who need and seek out the validation of someone else to feel good enough and loved fall into the trap of these emotionally avoidant love bombers who eventually pull away and trigger their hurt all over again. Perpetuating their own anxious cycle and solidifying their belief that they are not good enough, attractive enough or loveable enough.

In my own dating life, I reached a point where I timed myself out. And it's not because I'd had a raft of bad experiences or relationships. It's because I could see what I was attracting on repeat, and the dating washing machine I was putting myself in that wasn't giving me the relationship I hoped for. And in timing myself out, I saw something profound in my journey that I'd never realised or acknowledged before. I was a thirty-seven-year-old woman who hadn't been single or pursued her own thing without the distraction of a man's presence in her life or in her head since she was seventeen. I'd always had someone. This is huge for a woman to realise and has more impact on us than it does on men in the same position for several reasons.

In all of my long-term relationships, the man had been the stronger personality and the driver of our relationship. I had played second fiddle to them in many ways. I might have ruled the home, but outside of that, he was the decision maker, even in those joint couple decisions. I had very much followed lead. This is a masculine and feminine balance that exists in all relationships. Someone needs to take on each of these roles or share them. In a connected, loving relationship, this dynamic is actually beautiful. The masculine is the loving container that holds, leads, supports, cares for the feminine, which allows the feminine to bring the love, fun, spark, grace to the container and the relationship. But my dynamic meant that I hadn't had sovereignty over my own life and choices for almost twenty years. For twenty years I lived someone else's life set out for me. And here I was, finally, free but feeling out of my own depth and a little lost to find myself on my own for the first time in a long time. It was deeply triggering. As much as I knew it was where I needed to be, I found the time difficult to enjoy. Found it hard to enjoy the peace in the situation as much as I knew it was good for me.

There is a primal need for safety and security that we carry within us, a remnant from old times, where being chosen by someone meant we were going to be taken care of, fed and sheltered. It's right up there with our primal need to procreate. As powerful a driver too.

Choosing to be on my own for a time and to not date anyone unless they ticked all of the boxes allowed me to see just how much validation and safety I felt in having a man choose me. The degree of triggering to realise this was huge. You are enough, Carla, even though you are not engaging with a single male on the planet right now, even though no interested man is really showing up for you on your phone or at your doorstep. You are enough. And you are safe and secure, my dear inner cave woman with how life is right now. You don't need to trigger me to go out and seek safety and security in a man. I have my own safety and security. I don't need to find it solely in a man but thank you for looking out for me. I desire love, connection and laugher, things that life didn't grace you with the opportunity to seek. We've got this.

Life is a mirror to our healed and unhealed parts, and so the beauty and magic of doing the work on ourselves is this: not only does it benefit us, bring us peace and lift our personal vibration, it also in turn magnetises in our life partners who are of the same energetic vibration as us. Sometimes a big old timeout brings clarity, baby! It allows us to see the forest beyond the trees. And it will go on to change the trajectory of your life and your future relationships. Believe it!

13
OUR QUEEN LIFE PATH, WHAT IS IT

She's you with your crown firmly on. Like you've never worn it before. Owning your self-worth, sexually confident in your own skin and body, mastering your energy, choosing consciously for yourself what you desire, seeing your potential and finding yourself a partner that is an energetic, vibrational match for who you are now.

WHY I USE THE TERM: QUEEN LIFE PATH.

This absolutely is a loving alter ego of you, a powerful one. Sometimes when we forget who we are, we really have to throw every part of ourselves into believing in that inner being before we're feeling it or have even met her. The people whose energy you admire, and love are not better than you, they are simply living life as their fullest self-expression.

Their Queen Life Path is lit up. They're walking it.

Let that sink in. It's not that you can't. It's believing that you can't that's holding you back. Most people live life to a small percentage of who they are. They hold back the parts of themselves that would allow them to shine their own version of magic onto the world. They stay small. They shy away from showing up in all their magnificence. The queen or the princess, which is the essence that you embody and move through life (and love) with?

QUEEN AND PRINCESS ENERGY

Princess
- Compares herself to others and often feels not good enough and tries to hide this. Can tend to change her personality and essence for others. Guarded. Wishes someone would love her for her, not realising she never lets anyone see, feel or taste the real her.
- Moves more from her wounds than she does her heart. She is cautious and closed. She can be needy and seeks attention through her behaviour. He will find her presence initially fun but will feel more drama and a loss of freedom over time because of this type of connection.
- Intuition is often dismissed and drowned out. Not connected with her feminine energy and intuitive gifts. Therefore, she can't trust herself.
- Unsure of her value. Unsure of her worth and seeks reassurance from external validation—desire and attention from others. Does entertain boys.
- Her life path is solely focused on finding a partner or having a partner. The enthusiasm for her life path diminishes entirely when she has a partner.
- Is hooked in by toxic, push/pull and negative behaviours.
- A need to prove her worth, that she is good enough.
- Is more trained in opening herself up physically with someone before she shares her full essence and personality. Not comfortable with being seen. Sex first or early. Soul connection second.

Queen
- Accepts herself and is confident, comfortable in her personality and own skin. Comfortable with being seen as the full essence of herself. No pretence or show.
- Has the space, time and relaxed energy for a good man when he shows up in her life but isn't defined by his presence or lack thereof. He will find her presence nourishing, open, fun and playful.
- Follows and listens to her intuition. High degree of self-trust. A knowingness.
- Owns her value. Knows her worth. Protective of both. Doesn't entertain boys. Boys typically don't try it on.
- Has her own life path going on whether she is single or in a relationship.
- Doesn't concern herself with inconsistency, confusion, push/pull, hot/cold, low-effort nonsense.
- Free in her full sexual expression and energy in spaces where she feels trust and respect. Sex is a means of deeper connection and expressing herself with another. Sex is not the connection. Wants to be seen and only seeks out those able to see her.

Learning to be the queen of my life has been a journey of finding my confidence, of owning my path, self-expression and worth. It has transformed my life and relationships. I wasn't always on this path, I am now. I am in alignment with myself, which allows me to attract into my life everything that aligns with the real me, the highest-self version of me. I walk my path knowing it is me in my fullest essence, and I expect, trust and know that what is meant for me will come to me on my path. I don't need to force, manipulate, chase. Something or someone is either meant for me or they are not. And if they are meant for me later, staying true to my path will allow them to circle back for me. I have my intention. I know where I am going. I am conscious of how I want to feel in my life and in myself and my role is to stay beautifully on this path. Magnetic. Happy. Living life as my best self. As rarely distracted from my path as I can manage. That is all.

Once you find this place within yourself, you never really go back. And you begin to become very good at recognising who or what is taking you away from your life path or who is beautifully adding to it. Life becomes very clear. Clearer than it's ever been. And your role in it becomes clear, clearer than it's ever been. Queen energy is the rudder that steers my path. This energy comes completely from within. It has nothing to do with how we dress or present or what we say. I am so grateful that the important men in my family and life have always celebrated and encouraged the queen energy in me.

There is nothing to stop you from starting to live and move through life in this same way. In fact, I wish for you to start now. I can say, as a woman who moves primarily with this queen energy (we all carry a little princess on the inside, she never fully leaves us!), that it's defining to have, not just in love but in life. I wish it for all women.

Ask yourself, what are you not expressing and sharing with the world? What are you not doing in life right now that you should be embracing and running towards with enthusiasm? What is your Queen Life Path that you're not owning and walking?

This path, when you walk it, will change everything for you.

14

WHY DO WE AVOID FULLY OWNING AND LIVING OUR QUEEN LIFE PATH

Let's own something outright, right now. We are the first generation of women to have the privilege and opportunity to be the queen of our own lives with or without a king by our side. Collectively, this is new for us as women. And let's extend a little compassion out into the world in this moment too. This change in our dynamic is also new for men. Both sexes are wondering what to do with this change in balance right now and how it looks. Men are not feeling appreciated for actions and behaviours that were enough in previous generations. And women now want to be loved (not just provided for), to have their own lives, to have opportunities outside of the home and for our growth to be equally supported and encouraged. But let's be honest here with ourselves too. As women, we may desire this path, but the majority of us are not fully owning it! What a discord of mixed messaging to the masculine we are sending: Treat me like a queen, but can you save me like a princess too?

In previous generations, marriage was as much a transactional exchange as it was a love and family bond, if you were blessed to have that. One earnt the income to support the family, typically the man. One took care of the home and the children, typically the woman. And that's just how it was. The crossing over of roles has intensified in the last forty to fifty years more than ever, especially with the rise of women entering the workforce, changes in divorce laws and evolving societal expectations. Now we expect and need both from both sexes. So why do we as women shy away from owning and walking our Queen Life Path enthusiastically and with gusto? Especially when it is so clearly the smartest pathway to lead us out of this current change in the masculine and feminine balance. Quite simply, we're used to being tied to the kitchen sink and in many ways co-dependent. There are few females in previous generations who modelled to us what living our Queen Life Path looked like while still having a family and a loving relationship. Our safety and security, those primal needs again, came almost fully from our roles of caregiver and nurturer within the household. To step outside of those roles in past generations was to be too much and to ask for too much. Safer for us to stay within the limits of our roles and our place.

We are literally the first in our female lineage to walk our Queen Life Path with this much freedom as we do. I will break many, many years of female conditioning if I can be at my fullest self-expression, loving my life, and be in a supportive container of a relationship that I've consciously chosen that happily holds and loves all of me.

I was graced with some beautiful great-aunts who I was blessed to know into my teens: Auntie Bea, Auntie Shirl and Aunt Mabel (who I never personally met, but whose tales I heard all about). All were born in the late 1800s to early 1900s and lived well into their nineties. They were gutsy, fiery, beautifully poised women who dressed immaculately and were full of wit, but who chose early on in their life to never marry or have children because of the cost that doing either would have on their life and independence. The aunts went on to be school headmistresses, work and travel overseas, play golf, live together into their old age, do as they please with their time and kept no man in their life who went past boyfriend or lover, aside from Aunt Mabel, who went on to marry in her sixties.

We don't need to make those same choices and sacrifices as women today to keep our independence and freedom. We get to have it all. Maybe not all at once, but we do get to have it all. We can have a career and have children. We can have a husband and decide for ourselves if we want to continue working or not outside of the home. Getting married for us does not equal automatically housebound woman as it did for my great-aunts. And for this I am grateful. Very grateful.

So, whenever I have had a moment of self-doubt and fear as I've walked my Queen Life Path, whenever I've felt like a small rope is tied around my foot, questioned my next step forward, slowed down or questioned myself as I've walked along my path, wondering where I'm going or how this is all going to come together for me, I have thought about my great-aunts. I think about how much they would have loved to be walking and journeying in my shoes. How much they'd have loved the freedom to choose everything they pleased. *Run with it*, is what they'd wish for me. And so, I go again, knowing I bring others with me from my past and present when I do.

And so should you, for the women in your ancestral lines who would have loved to be where you are today, doing what you do, with the choices that you have in front of you that they could never have imagined for themselves. Own your Queen Life Path as much as those ladies in your ancestral lines would love to see you own it.

15
WOMEN SET THE TONE

A friend and matchmaker, Louanne Ward, shared a brilliant truism with me one day: 'Women can be taught but they can't be trained. Men can be trained but they can't be taught.' The statement made me laugh for its political incorrectness, but any woman would agree, this feels very much true. Whether it's a man or woman. What we accept from others in their behaviour is either enabling them or training them to treat us in a certain way. We are enabling them and allowing them to get away with less-than-ideal behaviour. To stay the same or slowly worsen over time. Or are we training them on how we want them to be loved, held and appreciated. What we will accept. Women set the tone. The boundaries are our own. So are our standards. And when we compromise on these, we are letting men set the tone. Compromise is a beautiful thing. But not when it comes to the tone of a relationship.

Lift the bar please ladies and keep it there. Praise and shine light on the behaviour you love, good men want to please us and want to feel needed and appreciated. Give less attention, turn your back and don't chase behaviour that isn't deserving of you. Set the tone of your life and relationships knowing that this will either raise the consciousness of your partner or it won't. That's their life path and their journey. Not your own.

16
LIFE IS A PROCESS OF LEVELLING UP

The job, the relationship, the situation you're leaving is something someone else is manifesting into their life. Your next is someone else's outgrown. What you're moving on from is someone else's dream. What a wonderful series of sliding doors where we are the only thing that is truly getting in the way of the process. When we get this, we get life at its essence. We understand its process. Life truly is a series of up-levels. When we understand this, we see that the only commonality between the levels is ourselves. It is us that have kept ourselves stuck in the past. And it is us who is doing it in the present moment and into the future.

Living with a Queen Life Path, you level up your perception and beliefs about yourself might feel like an entirely new way of thinking and living. And if this is the case, then it might feel uncomfortable at times. Too much, almost. Welcome to your first up-level of owning what you really want, taking up a little more space than you used to and trusting that everything meant for you will come when it's meant to. Where we desire to go next, what we believe we are worthy of having next all sits ahead of us on the horizon.

A space is always being created for your 'next' to step and evolve into. Life always delivers something else that's wonderful when we move forward with this energy. Trust and have faith. Let yourself rise, sister, rise. Expand brilliantly instead of contracting in your life now.

17
FOR THOSE WHO SUFFERED EMOTIONAL ABUSE

If this is you, I want you to know, I see you and hear you more than you know. And so, I ask of you. Please stop downplaying the wounds and trauma that taking emotional and toxic blows has inflicted on your soul and spirit. Please stop moving through life as though they're not there. Please stop acting like they're not affecting your future life experiences, beliefs about yourself and choices like they are. It's a cruel analogy to use but at least when someone punches you in the face, there is no hiding the bruises and trauma they have left you with. You can visually see it. The abuser can't twist it, deny it, turn it back on you or downplay what has just unfolded with words like: 'Not a big deal. Why are you still thinking about that? Why aren't you over that already? I never said that.' It would be there for everyone, including them, to see. Imagine every emotional blow landing on you as though it had been a physical one. Physical bruises last longer than the moment they're made, so do emotional ones. If you're experiencing emotional abuse or have experienced it in the past, please don't fall into their behaviour trap of downplaying the deep effect this has had on your soul. Seek professional help. Please give yourself the same kindness and healing you would gift someone dealing with physical abuse if they were to stand in front of you. Others may not see your bruises, physically you also can't see them, but that doesn't mean they're not there.

> *In no way do I intend to downplay physical abuse or domestic violence in this chapter. I intend to only bring light to the emotional abuse people suffer with, often silently, also.*

18
WHAT TO EXPECT WHEN YOU GO AND CHANGE THE BOUNDARIES ON YOUR EX

Know that when changing your boundaries, not everyone is necessarily going to be happy for you. Stay with it anyway. And this might apply to your ex for a time. When you change the rules on him, what you used to accept from him in words, actions and behaviour you no longer do, have to or want to. Changing the rules on someone in regard to how we expect to be treated and spoken to usually elicits:

- A push back.
- A 'how dare you treat me, speak to me like this' response.
- A 'who do you think you are' response.
- Further and greater attempts than ever to undermine, control or bully you back into your 'place' where they're used to you being.

This is almost always about control and ego. Throw them some love, light and healing and a shit tonne of compassion. They're adjusting to a new version of you, and they don't know how to handle her. Energetically, they can feel you pulling away even if they don't realise that they do.

Celebrate your personal growth here; you have already risen above where you used to be, even if you're still finding your feet in this new space. Expand into this new place anyway but do take steps to protect yourself with greater emotional or physical space away from them if you need it. Leave space for the dust to settle and own that, in some way, your behaviour did enable him to be like this, which means that this is simply part of the fallout. A lesson in keeping our standards high, to not lower them and to maintain this tone into our future. Gift them the opportunity to adjust (or not). Do continue to trust in your own path and self-growth. Continue to value your self-worth. You've got this, queen, whether they like who you are now or not, agree with it or not.

19
SELF-REFLECTION IS OFTEN AN ARSE, BUT WE CAN'T AVOID IT

While I was writing this book, a girlfriend asked, 'This book you're writing, who is it for?' I told her it's for the woman who has left a long-term relationship and doesn't realise the self-journey ahead of her. Who doesn't want to hear about the necessary healing and inner work ahead of her and just wants to dive into her next happily-ever-after relationship. And we both laughed because when we left our marriages, we'd both felt like that too. We both had hoped for the immediate happily-ever-after story. We were that woman. Blissfully unaware of what the journey ahead was really going to be about. More interested in finding our next someone who would love us and make it all better. We left our marriages wanting love and that's what we sought out in the world. Never really thinking too much about the love we needed to seek within ourselves first. Both of us had done 'work' on ourselves leading up to our marriages ending. But really, looking back, we were asleep to the true healing and self-reflection work that we needed to do on ourselves.

I remember seeing a well-regarded psychic just before leaving my marriage. And like a good psychic, she saw it all. Saw me leaving and was unequivocal in telling me that it was the right thing to do. And then she looked into my future. She told me that it would take me five years to meet the right man for me because I had so much growing-up and work to do on myself. When she told me this, I thought she was wrong. I can do better than that. It won't take me that long. Psychics are often wrong. And I really tried to prove her wrong. Believe me. I did my absolute best.

In those five years, I did grow and evolve. Even though I hadn't been seeking that journey, it was the journey I walked. I truly stepped into my own as a woman during this time, for the first time ever. And I had several long-term relationships with men who were fully supportive of my growth and journey. Including a marriage proposal. Relationships that on paper could have been my full stop. One in particular, I assumed was going to be my forever. Yet I outgrew every one of them. Either I left them, or they left me because they knew they couldn't give me what I was ready for. The heartbreak and loss was real during this time. I was growing and evolving naturally, but I was continually and heartbreakingly outgrowing love along the way. I knew I was on the right path for me, that I was unfolding and blossoming naturally into my full self simply through the process of living my life. The only thing missing was that love still wasn't in my life in the way I desired.

The self-reflection was deep. Hand on heart, I can tell you that almost every time I didn't want to see the gaps within myself mirrored back to me in such a way. I just wanted to be there already. To be healed. Whether we ask for it or not, want it or not, the self-reflection will come. If you're reading this book, you're a conscious, growth-minded and beautiful soul. And so, self-reflection is going to be part of your journey. It is divine that you are reading this book. It tells me that you live life more from your heart than you do your head. So many people are the opposite, which is why they find themselves stuck and cycling in situations that feel unfulfilled. Their logic outweighs their feelings. Actually, that is the upside-down way to live. Because your logic can never fully silence how you feel. However much you try. In life, we should lead from our heart, and it is our head that should follow. Not the other way round. Can you see and feel the different lives that leading with each one brings?

I lived very much from my head during much of my marriage. Leaving my marriage was me beginning to listen and move from my heart again. My heart was in the driver's seat. My heart was in the lead. My head booted to the passenger's side. Part of my journey has been learning to trust myself and to trust life in a way that allows my heart to stay open and to lead from that place. If I could have a conversation with my younger self straight after she left her marriage, in the driver's seat of her life, feeling like she was going one hundred kilometres an hour but actually going five kilometres an hour with a cocktail in hand, wearing her hot new wardrobe, I would say to her:

> *Enjoy the journey more.*
> *Stay in your heart and follow your feelings.*
> *That's your beauty and what makes you magnetic.*
>
> *Everything in your own time.*
> *Just because it isn't here now doesn't mean it's not on its way.*
>
> *Trust yourself, girl. Stay always open to life.*
> *Embrace all that life reflects back to you about yourself and seek out a professional to heal yourself.*

I would ask her to take the time to embody everything she has learnt about herself before she throws herself into the next thing or someone. I would tell her:

> *Your broken heart is actually your most open heart; let that light shine in when heartbreak happens. That's when the transformation occurs. Don't hide from it.*

Self-reflection after a divorce is an arse. It brings up all the questions and regrets that we sometimes don't want to face and that we perhaps didn't even know were there. Why didn't I leave sooner? Why did he leave me? Why do I fear that happening for me in the future? What's wrong with me? All I want you to know is this. Your answers won't all come at once. Your answers will continue to evolve. The layers of the onion will reveal themselves as you live your life. The work is never actually done. It just keeps happening around us.

Let your shields down when life mirrors back to you your wounds and guardedness. Let yourself sit with what this means. Because we all carry these protective shields, it's what we do with them next that matters. Lower them or keep them up. Stay open to getting to know your inner workings more. Keep doing you. Heal, don't hide.

20
THE THOUGHT OF BEING NAKED WITH SOMEONE ELSE

It's a block for many women. Sometimes the thought of being naked with someone else is too much to even think about. This is more likely to be true if you were the one who was pushed rather than the one who willingly jumped. There is a certain feeling of safety that comes with one man who we loved being the only one we opened our bodies up to over a long period of time. The beautiful joy of the sacredness that is being a divine woman. Ours is truly a receiving and letting-in energy, physically and energetically. The old adage of the best way to get over a man is to get under another one, isn't always true here.

I won't lie. Yes, it can sometimes feel like ripping off a Band-Aid to move on physically like this. It's done. The person we just left or who left us feels cancelled out and we feel empowered, temporarily, anyway. But the temporarily is the thing. Everyone's beliefs here are going to look and feel different and that's okay. What's right for one is not necessarily right for another. No judgement here on any woman and how she chooses to move with her body and soul. But my belief here is that we should only open ourselves up to someone physically when we are truly ready to be seen and truly ready to let someone into our body.

I've had experiences where I have dived into another relationship (or fling) to cancel out the one I just left. Trying to make the process of moving on from him faster. It never ended well for me. I ended up in rebound relationships that were not meant for me. And I hurt people in the process. Men catch feelings too, as easily as women do.

Opening ourselves up to being naked and sensual with our bodies again with another man will bring with it a different timeline for every woman. There is a big difference between being naked and having sex with a man and being naked and sensually open to a man who is fully enjoying you while you are enjoying them. This process might look like learning to love your own body for a time because your body is different from the body you had the last time you were dating.

Self-pleasure is important here, especially if you have left a marriage that felt loveless and was lacking in intimacy for quite some time. Especially if you haven't had a full-body orgasm in a long time, whether with your ex or on your own. An orgasm is connected to your level of emotional openness. So, if you have been in any way emotionally traumatised or repressed, now is the time to explore and deepen into moving yourself out of this.

Embrace your nakedness again and relish in your body for who she is today. Have massages, do nude yoga, anything that allows you to connect with your own body and its innate beauty and power. You are a woman, and your body is ready to be loved, honoured and adored. But that journey starts with you first.

21
IT TAKES TWO TO BE TOXIC

This can be a bitter pill to swallow. I invite you to sit with it because at a point in your life, you chose your partner. No one forced you to be with him. You chose him. And this means your relationship together was as much a reflection of him as it was you. Whoever might feel more wronged or abandoned, this statement is still true. Sorry. It's not me. It's not you. It was us.

When we project our blame onto others, we avoid the necessary process of self-reflection. The truth is that it always takes two. Just like tennis, one hits the ball over the net from their side and someone always hit it back. It only stops when someone puts down their racket and refuses to play anymore. Looking at all the ways we returned the ball over the net to continue allowing this game to play out is powerful. How someone chooses to show up is their business. How you show up is yours. Always own yours. Leave others to do as they please with theirs. If you were hooked on the drama and the push/pull nature, as uncomfortable as it is to admit, own it. If you ignored your intuition and turned a blind eye so you could continue playing this game, own it. If you self-abandoned by downplaying and ignoring your own needs and feelings, own it.

Own it, whatever it was. And consciously choose to do better and different next time. It always takes two for a relationship to be toxic. It couldn't have been a relationship otherwise. You must own your part.

22
I DON'T WANT TO BE SAVED BY A MAN, BUT WHERE DO I START SAVING MYSELF

The fears I hear. One privilege of working with women in this space and season in their life is the commonalities I hear. All of the fears, thoughts and self-doubts that once had you afraid to leave your marriage are also the gateway to understanding where you need to save yourself, where you need to feel more safe and secure within. You've got this, more than you know. As you move forward, you will begin proving it to yourself as life falls into place around you. When we make space and then set an intention, life always responds. Life stops responding only when we stop. Facing our deepest fears and limitations, willingly shining a big light on them, is the beginning process of knowing this is where I need to go within, this is what I need to embrace more of.

What I was hearing:
I will struggle financially and completely lose the lifestyle that I love.

What I wish I was hearing:
What a wonderful way to learn to be financially independent and empowered and to create a life that feels as good behind closed doors as it looks. I have time to recreate this lifestyle for myself whether on my own or with someone else in time.

I need to find my own confidence and learnings around money.

What I was hearing:
No one will love me. I won't find love again.

What I wish I was hearing:
I've found loved before, of course I will find love again. This next time will be amazing and more aligned for me than ever.

I need to love and value myself more. I need to appreciate myself more for my own beauty and gifts.

What I was hearing:
This will hurt my children. I am selfish to choose my own happiness over theirs.

What I wish I was hearing:
What a beautiful way to demonstrate to my children what love looks like so they don't end up in a relationship like ours and instead will go on to choose healthier, more loving relationships for themselves. My children learn what love looks like by watching me live my life, not by listening to me.

I need to discover who I am as a woman now—whole, fulfilled, lit up and loving my each and every beautiful day.

What I was hearing:
The grass isn't greener on the other side of the fence. It won't be any better with someone else.

What I wish I was hearing:
I'm using the 'grass isn't greener' line to keep myself safe and I am abandoning my true feelings to do so. What I desire isn't being fulfilled in this relationship. If other people can enjoy relationships and dynamics like I desire, then so can I.

I need to live my life more from a place of honouring my own needs and desires over needing to please others. This doesn't make me selfish or too much. This makes me beautifully human. I move through life from my heart, not from my head.

What I was hearing:
Who will want me or love me with so many children/such young children?

What I wish I was hearing:
The right person will love and welcome my children because he loves me and he won't want to lose me. My children are an extension of me, of course they will be loved.

I need to embrace my children and family as one of the most beautiful parts of me and what I have to offer someone. Family is everything to me and will be the same to any future partner that comes into my life.

23

I WAS CELIBATE FOR TWELVE MONTHS AND THIS IS WHAT I LEARNT

Before this I hadn't had a one-night stand since I was nineteen. It just didn't do it for me. I don't judge anyone who does do this. I was a relationship person. I always found myself in one. Being celibate for twelve months wasn't something I intentionally set out to do. It just happened and time just passed. I left a relationship that I thought was going to be my forever and then my grandad passed away. Both happening within weeks of one another.

The complete pain of losing two big men in my life like that made me do something I'd never had to do before in my life. I completely stopped. I was lost. Numb. Feeling more alone than ever. Abandoned. These twelve months showed me how much I was still used to moving from this place of needing to be saved. How daunting it felt to go against this and to cultivate a sense of safety and security for myself. Independent of a man.

For twelve months, if it wasn't a soul that deeply grabbed me, I didn't pursue it. I came to realise how few true soul-to-soul connections we really do have in our life. How so many of my past ones were more noise than soul. How they had been a distraction from me walking and owning my path. From me owning my strengths, beauty and gifts. In this time, I became the full creator of my own life. I owned my life path, and I walked it solo… for the first time, with no one holding my hand. I found my own safety and security within myself and realised how much of that I'd received from my grandad in my past. How much I had received from my ex-boyfriend that I'd recently left. It was so hugely triggering. But the beauty from this time was profound.

My business almost tripled. My self-growth, confidence and transformation exploded. My self-worth grew. My personal relationships blossomed. I started swimming and found a new life love. I had given so much of my own power away because I had shied away from fully owning all of myself. Shied away from being confident and capable on my own. Walking solo for a time finally allowed me to find and embody this. And now I have her back. I found myself in a completely new space in myself and in my life. I don't recommend this for everyone. I never place timelines on such things. And there are no things we must do in life. But for you if this inspires. Create this time for yourself, just like I did. It will open your eyes up to something about yourself.

24
MY MONEY STORY

I am the eldest child of four. Two brothers and one half-sister. I am a cruise-ship baby. My mother was on her first overseas holiday as a nineteen-year-old on the P&O *Fairstar* when she accidentally fell pregnant with me. My dad was a ship steward. He was Portuguese and had recently left the Portuguese army after being conscripted and doing the compulsory time. He was loving the cruise ship and island life. He also could barely speak any English.

I was named after the black Carla Zampatti dress that my mum was wearing on the night I was conceived. Thigh-high split. Deep V-neck that nearly reached the split. You get the picture. On returning home and discovering that she was pregnant, my mum went back on the same cruise to find Dad and let him know that I was coming into the world—knowing she would find my dad, still being a ship steward and circling the islands of Vanuatu and Fiji. And just like that, with the aid of an English interpreter, they docked in Sydney and were married straight away for the sake of Dad's visa. My mum was seven months pregnant on her wedding day and no longer able to fit into the Carla Zampatti dress.

They moved into a caravan in the backyard of my grandparent's place in Tasmania, while they found their feet financially, and while Dad learnt English so he could find work outside of fruit and vegetable picking. My parents were married for fourteen years and considering where they started, and what they started with, they did amazing. My childhood was loving. Dad made lots of Portuguese-speaking friends and life, in my eyes as a child, was good. We lived on three acres, Dad had a hobby vineyard, Mum shopped at the local designer store and was always trying new dishes and expanding her recipe journal. Looking back over old home videos set to music by the Gypsy Kings and Dire Straits, we were more wog than I realised. It had never occurred to me that not everybody had fresh sardines on their barbecue or bacalhau as a staple dish. Certainly, this wasn't normal for the nineties in Tasmania, in a small town so far from being multicultural that the only Chinese people in town were the ones who owned the Chinese restaurant.

Life was mostly good until my parents divorced when I was fourteen. And before life became mostly good again, for a couple of years it wasn't so much. My parents' divorce wasn't all that civilised, and through events outside of my own doing and because of choices I made that were best for me at the time, my parents' divorce eventually ended up costing me my relationship with my father. Despite our best attempts before he died, I never spoke to my dad properly again without one of us yelling or getting frustrated. My mum, when she was married, had been the stay-at-home mum and only ever ventured out to work part-time when we were saving as a family to go overseas to visit Dad's family. And that's how I'd always known things. Dad worked. Mum stayed at home. But after my parents' divorce, Dad did the bitter thing, which in no way reflects the man he actually was and quit his office job at the local paper mill to open Tasmania's first handmade pasta takeaway shop. He started claiming his income at a loss and stopped paying Mum any real child support. This, among other things, was part of the reason we fell out. I caught Mum crying over the child-support forms one night. So much effort to fill them out, to only claim seven dollars a week from him. I remember her saying to me, you kids eat more than that in one breakfast.

I helped her fill out the forms that night, saying to her if Dad was going to lie about his income, then let him do it. When Dad found out about this was when he and I really fell out with each other for good. In his eyes, I was like my mum, and honestly, I didn't know what he was to me anymore at that time. My dad was a good man. A beautiful father. And I'm so sorry that he wasn't alive to meet my daughters when they arrived into the world because he would have made a loving grandfather and avô. But this is the story, and I have no doubt he'd do things differently if he had his time again.

To get by after her divorce, my mum took on three jobs, waitressing at two different places and cleaning hotel rooms. We went from seeing her all the time to seeing our grandparents and being at their house all the time. Thank God for them! One of the venues that Mum waitressed at held a lot of state functions and events. The menu was fancy. And the kitchen, knowing that Mum was struggling, would keep us all of their uneaten food. We might have been struggling financially during those years of Mum being divorced and single, but we ate like kings and queens on their leftovers. I took quail to school in my lunch box so many times that as an adult I never need to eat another small bird ever again. My mum was single for two years before meeting my stepdad, Chris, and accidentally falling pregnant to him. And with Chris's entrance into our home and world, a man that was much loved and adored by all of us at the time, life almost returned to how it had been before the divorce.

Mum and Chris pooled their money together to buy a larger house, my mum stumping up more than Chris because of her financial settlement, and Mum gave birth to my half-sister, returning to her role that she loved and thrived in as a stay-at-home mum for all of us. And life was good again. She was around all the time again. Our garden was amazing. New recipes and dishes were flying out of the kitchen again and Mum even had time to vacuum the front verandah of our renovated federation home, which lit her up so much that one year we bought her a vacuum that she could wear on her back like a backpack. I love my mum. And I wouldn't change her for the world.

So much of our relationship with money is learnt through observing our parents' experience with it. What did my parents' experience with money teach me? That women struggled financially if they weren't in a relationship. That men could be selfish and overly protective with their money. That men were better with money than women. That men called the shots with money. That leaving a marriage equalled financial pain.

All of this I learnt as a child without realising it. Can you see how your childhood helped shape your own? When I hit year twelve in my schooling, I was desperate to have a gap year before starting university. My mum, happily raising my toddler half-sister, declared absolutely not. She didn't care what I did but I was to get a degree that would lead me to a job that paid well. I was so annoyed with my mother at the time but I'm so grateful that she gave me no choice. She wanted me to have the financial choices that she hadn't had. And for that, I'm forever grateful, because she completely changed my life trajectory in doing so.

I did the first year of an arts/psychology degree, hated it and failed it due to my lack of attendance at my philosophy tutorials. I changed degrees and moved interstate, having somehow spun myself a full fee-paying scholarship to the University of Melbourne, where I studied to become a dental hygienist. I didn't choose that career path because I loved teeth. I chose it because I'd been told that the job paid amazing and there was a shortage of dental hygienists in the workplace. I wanted freedom, I wanted flexibility, and I wanted to get the hell out of Tasmania. So I did.

Thank you to my mum, thank you to the universe, thank you to my life path for delivering me to a career that gave me options and financial stability. Something that not every woman is afforded. My mum and dad's financial experience certainly shaped my own. It shaped the career I chose for myself, the man I chose to marry because I could see so much love and financial security in him, not because he had money but because he was good with money. It led me to defer all of our financial plans to him during our marriage because I believed him to know more and be better at it than I, which he was at the time. And my financial story definitely kept me in an unhappy marriage, uncertain whether to leave or not, scared of how much my life would change financially if I ever were to leave.

When I left my marriage and passed through the emotional and triggering car crash that for me was separating our finances, I freaked out. I left with some money; for that I am very grateful because it gave me choices. But I was also a woman in her mid-thirties who had never been in charge of money on her own before, certainly not in charge successfully. I still remember standing at the mailbox of my new home after our divorce and opening my first electrical bill. It was the first time as an adult that I'd received a household bill with my name on it solely. Even with money in the bank, I had a mini meltdown realising that for the first time this was all on me to keep up with and on top of. Money continued to give me anxiety for many years to come. I wasn't sure what to do with it. I enjoyed spending it but felt guilty when I did. And I was forever fond of asking my boyfriends at the time—who, true to my type, were good with and better with money than I—for their feedback and opinions on any financial decision I was making.

Improving my mindset around money and feeling confident with money has been my thing that I have needed to save myself on. And it continues to be. Not because of a lack of it but because of my lower exposure and education to it. Yes, it has been life changing and important to change the love and types of men I attract into my life. So has been all the self-work I've done to really step into my fullest self-expression and worth. Still, my money journey remains the most important journey in my life that I've taken and continue to take. To own it, improve on it, to empower myself around the topic. Because ultimately, it was my poor money story that led me to make many of my past decisions in all those other areas of my life. I find this true for a lot of women. Rather than owning our own financial story and empowerment, we willingly handed it over.

Financial empowerment is less about the dollar amount that you are earning, less about the dollar amount in your bank, it's all about how much you believe you can earn. And what you do with it when you do. I'm so proud of myself for over time treading an almost different financial path as a single woman than my mother was able to. And I know she is proud of me too. Everything she did for me I have made the best of and made it work for me. I am only here because of what she pushed me to do and because of what she showed me accidentally, through living example, not to do. For that I'm grateful. I have become all that she was and all that she couldn't be. Every generation of women grows financially stronger than the last. I can't wait to see what my daughters do, having brought them up to this next step with me, to start creating their lives from.

25
LOVE IS RARE, MONEY IS EVERYWHERE

Financial fear. It's the biggest worry I hear that keeps men and women afraid to leave a marriage. I can't tell you how many times I've had someone say to me that they would have left years ago if they were in a better financial position, if they didn't stand to lose so much financially. For women, money equals lifestyle and safety. It is the fear of having to be financially independent on their own, often after having been the lower earner in the relationship. For men it is the change in lifestyle, yes, but also a loss of a perceived self to lose half of their asset pool. For men, money and what they've built up around them often feels like an extension of themselves, their success. It is often an extension of their ego. It's why a divorce can turn ugly so easily when finances are being discussed; carving up the asset pool is literally like taking a knife to some men's identity.

Love is rare. Money is everywhere. I said these words to a coaching client once during a session and they are true. Do you live more for love and emotional connection? Or do you live more for money? One can always be built back up, perhaps jointly with a beautiful new partner one day. One is special when it's found. Women, if your limitation was your finances, the only way out is to educate yourself and to improve your mindset around your earning potential. Stop looking to be saved in this area of your life, please. It is a skill to be learned, not a character flaw. You have it in you. And honestly, if I can learn it, without any real role modelling from women in my family, then so can you. Do as I did.

Seek out female friends who are clued up when it comes to their finances. Observe how they move through the world financially. How they talk about their financial life choices. And if you don't have female friends who move through life in this way, then seek out professional services or books for women around this topic. When we are empowered in this area of our life, our lives change, and our choices open up more than they ever have before. It's not about our purchasing power or what hangs in our wardrobe, but what we can say confident and clear yeses and noes too. This is true empowerment.

26

YOU'RE EITHER A WOMAN WITH A $3,000 HANDBAG OR A WOMAN WITH A $200 HANDBAG AND $2,800 IN THE BANK

I heard this statement at a women's financial event and the words have stuck in my mind ever since. Whether it's a fifty-dollar handbag or a two-hundred-dollar handbag, the differences in both women are quite profound. I don't judge either woman. I love the three-thousand-dollar handbags. But I don't own one. And anytime I've ever had a financial win and thought to buy one, I've thought on it and always pulled myself back. I'm sure that one day I will. But it will come from a place of having everything else absolutely in a line and my finances in excess.

As women, we are sold to every day. Most of us own so much stuff. But the truth is, we don't need as much of it as we think. Not like we feel we do. Tapping out of the world where shopping made me feel better or more of a confident version of myself, where how I looked and dressed was character defining, has changed me. Changed the kind of man I attract into my world too. The men around me now are also more financially aware and, dare I say it, grounded. Not every woman has to be like me, but you can still look good and have money in the bank. Honestly, I've never valued having money in the bank more than I do now. I'd much rather have it in the bank or in a house, over having it hang in my closet or on my arm.

This has been a real evolution of the way I handle my finances as a woman. A growing up. To embrace the word frugal but to still live an amazing life that is even deeper and more meaningful than before. To embrace less being absolutely more. To choose experiences over things. I move on belongings and items that I no longer wear like a queen and I'm very selective about what I bring in. This, in my eyes, is smart. And I'm so proud of myself for becoming this woman and continuing to grow into her.

27
WHATEVER YOU DO NEXT, MAKE SURE IT BRINGS YOU FUN

Whatever kind of love you're ready for next, when you feel ready to start looking, can we agree on one thing together? Let it be something that is fun and that makes you feel good. After everything you've been through, do you really have time and energy for anything or anyone that is draining, hard work or noncommittal? Did you really go through all you've been through for that? The answer should be a loud no. Can we agree on that, please?

28

WE DON'T MANIFEST THE END RESULT, WE MANIFEST EVERYTHING IN BETWEEN

There is an energetic vibration that matches where you are now and an energetic vibration that matches where you want to be. And quite possibly, there's a great difference between those two places and subsequent vibrations. The universe doesn't gift you what you want. It presents you with the next steps to help you arrive there. It is progressively trying to raise your vibration to the level of what it is that you want. So, you can not only have it but hold it. This goes for love. Your finances. Your career. Everything.

Everything you have and hold in your life will ascend higher in congruence with your level of growth and your capacity to expand into the energy of being able to hold with love and grace what it is that you seek. Very rarely do we just make a big leap, and often when we do we find ourselves self-sabotaging our good fortune and without meaning to, much like the lotto winners who within one to two years of winning millions of dollars find themselves poorer than they were before and with their most important relationships ruined. Energetically they had neither the skills nor the level of self-worth needed to hold, handle and appreciate that amount of money with grace.

Sending you something you're not an energetic vibration for yet is like pouring water into your hands, it would just slip through. In love this looks like Mr Perfect arriving at your front door, ready to love and hold you. Would you be ready for him if he entered your life today? Really? Or would you find yourself worrying that he was too good to be true? Waiting for him to leave you, see that you're not good enough or cheat on you? Whatever we want to come into our future, we need to learn how to become its energetic match first before we can hold it. Closing the gap between where we are now and where we desire to be. The first step forward towards manifesting anything is always the same. It's small.

29
TELL ME WHAT YOU WANT, WHAT YOU REALLY, REALLY WANT

You can't get to where you want to be if you don't know where it is that you want to be next. I'm all for going with the flow of life. It's how I live my life. I'm very much in flow. In my feminine. And I choose a lifestyle and relationships that support me to live in that way. I am also always intentional. I know where I'm going, though I have no real timeline on when it will unfold or expectations on how it will happen. And I know how I want to feel along the way.

A lot of my clients sit in front of me in our first session and admit this is one of their greatest struggles. To know what they want for themselves as a woman, now. Separate from anyone else's wants in life for them, separate from anyone else's intentions for them. Beautifully and simply their own. We don't have to have a grand vision of our life right now. We can simply know where we want to be next. I can't tell you how many times over the years that I've wished my journey to finding love and finding myself had been different. So many times. I won't lie to you and say this hasn't brought me sadness. It definitely has. It wasn't the path I imagined or wanted. But it is the one my soul needed. The truth is that if I had my time again, I wouldn't wish for anything different to have played out. It's all led me here. To be the woman that I am today. To be the mum that I am today. To be the lover I am today. To be the author and coach I am today, writing this for you. The experiences I've had along the way have been magic. I wouldn't be any of the above things today if I hadn't had the experiences that I have had. In fact, if I'd settled down and stayed with the first partner that I met after leaving my marriage, I would have stayed the same woman I was when I was married. And there would have been nothing wrong with that, only it's not who I am. Nor was it who I knew I could be.

So, I invite you to open your mind up to where you would love to be in one year. I'd love for you to think about how you'd love to feel in the next twelve months and to choose one guiding word that resonates deeply for you. Not a goal attached to a person or thing arriving in your life. A feeling. One that will act as your rudder for the next year. Visualise what you could do, achieve and experience in that time that would help you feel more of it in your life.

Your guiding word may change every few months. My words have varied from vibrant, supported, loved, adored, feminine, free. Every word matched an energetic point in my life at a time where that was the feeling I needed to feel and express. When we live intentionally from this place, we flow with life rather than force life. I liken this to allowing ourselves to be taken with the stream. We can't fight the flow; we can only go with it and remain mindful of how we want to feel along the way. The touch points we wish to experience as we move through. This is life. And we can either flow with it gracefully and easefully or we can resist it with control, fear, anxiety. I go for flow. I trust the flow of the stream to take me where I need to be; my intention is to simply feel amazing and do my best as I flow with it.

There is fate, there is destiny, there is free will and then there is the magic dance between all three. I believe in all three, though spiritual teachers will tell you that when you're moving with your free will, this is actually you following your destiny. What is meant for you will never pass you. What and who you need next will always present itself to you. Choose to know how you want to feel along the way. Choose to have experiences that will allow you to hold even more of this feeling and energy. Bloom and blossom in your life enthusiastically.

30

BALANCING OUR FEMININE AND MASCULINE ENERGIES TO ATTRACT LOVE AND TRUE HAPPINESS

When I look around, I see many women aching for love, appreciation and support. They want to attract more of that energy into their world. Women now have more opportunity, independence and choice than ever before, but many are more unfulfilled and disconnected than ever in personal relationships. We are tired of doing it all or feeling like we are. My intention is that this chapter will have you questioning everything you have been taught about what it means to embrace your femininity to attract love. That it will help you embrace softness and vulnerability so you can stop living with a guarded heart and the façade of I'm strong and have it *all* together. My hope is that it will also help you move into a space of flow and away from feeling the need to push or control to make things happen. I'm so passionate about this topic because I spent so many years feeling disconnected from myself, I was unhappy. Unhappy in myself. Unhappy in my marriage.

For me, leaving my marriage was the catalyst for finally being honest with myself and with others that while I had been living as though everything was fine, the truth was that everything was not fine and hadn't been for some time. After my separation, much of my energy was spent on being self-sufficient and independent, the necessary life stuff that we all need to embrace as part of the separating process. I was paying the bills on my own for the first time, parenting, keeping house, working full-time and building my business. I wanted a man, but I didn't want to need one. And I was intent on any man coming into my life knowing that. But I was living a half lie, because under it all I was exhausted and felt so alone. Even though I was dating someone.

At this time in my life, I was completely disconnected from myself and from my feminine. I was living in my head and not from my heart. I was always in my masculine energy of doing and rarely in my feminine energy of being.

THE FEMININE AND MASCULINE OUT OF BALANCE
Wounded feminine
- Afraid to speak her truth
- Lacks self-worth
- Tolerates toxic people
- Seeks external validation
- People-pleasers
- Apologises for who she is
- Has predominantly negative self-talk
- Compares herself to other women and sees them as competition
- Closed and disconnected from herself and her body

Wounded masculine
- Thinks vulnerability is weakness
- Lives in his head
- Numbs his feelings by focusing on porn, sex, money and power
- Seeks to control and dominate others
- Represses anger and trauma
- Justifies his anger
- Avoidant

I've come to learn is how important it is for women to embrace more of their feminine energy in its healthy, unwounded form. How much more fulfilled and centred we feel on the inside when we live and move from that place. How it changes everything that we attract into our world when we do. The love we attract. The friends we keep. The lifestyles we live. Literally everything changes. All women are both with an innate feminine essence and energy, trusting, loving, soft, playful, vulnerable. Simply, life and the experiences we have had since have made us otherwise. All of us carry both masculine and feminine energies. It's important to know that the balance of masculine and feminine varies in all of us. All of us move between the two depending on the task we're knee-deep in or what is on our mind at the time. So, we do need to learn to dance between these two energies successfully in our everyday life. This energy shapes who we are attracted to, how we perceive each other, and what we draw into our lives.

Which of the four predominant energies do you move through life with at your core? The healthy or unhealthy masculine? The healthy or unhealthy feminine?

THE FEMININE AND MASCULINE IN BALANCE
Divine feminine
- Honours her truth, her feelings and speaks it
- Knows her worth
- Sets loving boundaries
- Feels validated from within
- Inspires others to shine
- Lives unapologetically
- Speaks gently to herself
- Embodies her divine goddess and encourages other women to rise with her
- Intimacy killer: Feeling unseen, unsafe or misunderstood. A man who creates a push/pull energy in their relationship

Divine masculine
- Lives in his heart
- Doesn't fear vulnerability
- Embraces his feelings and his strengths
- Communicates clearly
- Seeks to understand himself and others
- Makes big things feel small
- Honours both the masculine and feminine energies
- Takes responsibility for his actions
- Intimacy killer: Being criticised, controlled or shut out. A woman not in touch with herself

Since the feminism-era, men and women have rejected aspects of their masculinity and femininity to avoid being perceived as dependent and helpless or macho, respectively. I had disowned aspects of my feminine self because I saw embracing them as weak and an invitation for a man to hurt me again. I was much more comfortable and confident in being seen in my masculine persona: strong, together, independent and capable. Heaven help the guy who was dating me at the time and just wanted to love me and be there for me unconditionally… he didn't stand a chance! In this masculine space, I pushed people away who didn't deserve to be pushed away, and for a time I attracted men who were emotionally unavailable, who didn't know what they wanted or who weren't relationship-ready. It was this experience that made me start to reflect on how I was moving through the world and acknowledge that maybe it said as much about me as it did them. Damn that! I realised that in being so independent, I was attracting men into my space who were actually being respectful of and admired my independence. They had no desire to impede on what I had going on or to be there for me, that was part of the attraction for them. They liked that I was so overly independent and together. It told them energetically that I wasn't looking for a man to fully show up for me. I had it sorted, or at least I acted like I did.

I want you to imagine for a moment a seesaw with each side equalling fifty per cent when in balance. The two together always having to equal one-hundred per cent. I realised I was overly in my masculine space and out of balance, sitting high up on the top of the seesaw; let's just say I was eighty per cent showing up in my masculine energy, so most of the time. It meant any man who chose to sit on the lower end of the seesaw had to be comfortable only being twenty per cent in his masculine; he would need to be more in his feminine energy to want to sit there. While teetering on the top of my seesaw, I realised several things. I wasn't moving through life as the woman I wanted to be and knew I could be. I was tired of doing it all, the sex was lacklustre up there, connections and love with others never felt genuine and deep, and on top of it all I felt like a fake, behaving like I was all good when I wasn't. I was lonely and tired. I was tired of being go-go-go all the time. I felt far from peaceful and at ease in myself. And I came to realise that I needed to lower my side of the seesaw closer down to fifty per cent to allow and make space for the masculine man I knew was a true match for who I was on the inside. I had to let my walls and my defences down. And as I did, dropping into and embracing more of my feminine side and energy, the men I started to attract, who started to show up and take a seat on the other side of the seesaw, started to change. Men in a healthy masculine place who knew what they wanted, who were respectful, who wanted to see me happy and fulfilled now had space to sit down and were choosing to sit down and stay on the seesaw. The other men I used to attract—the unavailable, the emotionally wounded who needed saving or were just looking for sex—stopped approaching me altogether or I wasn't interested in them.

WHY IS IT IMPORTANT THAT WE GET TO THIS PLACE IF WE WANT LOVE AND HAPPINESS?

Because we want a life and love that fills up our cup over one that empties it. For women, this is when we feel our most content, we feel loved for all the wild parts of us, heard and safe. We have more spirit and energy when we're in this place of balanced feminine energy on the seesaw. And men sitting in front of us in their balanced masculine energy feel their full selves, appreciated, needed and free. A woman living in her feminine energy longs to connect with what's around her. She wants relationship. She thrives on being more than she does doing. She wants love and to be loved.

I have a well-developed masculine energy, I love to succeed in my business and be the driver, and I enjoy life when I accomplish my goals. However, my deepest longing is for intimate relationships and connection. Life without those two things might look successful on the outside but it would feel empty on the inside. When I was honest with myself and got out of my own masculine way, admitting without shame what was missing in my life, I began to invite it in. I learnt to be predominantly in my feminine energy in my life. And I learnt how to be in my masculine energy when life needed it from me to achieve and get things done. Most importantly, I learnt to park that energy when I was done.

So how do we embrace living more in our feminine energy within a busy world? A world that often supports and needs us to be more in our masculine, succeeding and earning, thinking more over feeling, hiding over letting someone in to love us again?

31
A WOMAN ONLY HAS ROOM FOR ONE KING IN HER HEART

The king in your heart should be your partner. That makes sense if you're the queen. But for this little girl, the king in my heart had always been my grandad. When my dad left my life when I was fourteen, my grandad stepped in, and I found this kindred spirit within him. He started driving me around in his little two-seater van, full of machinery and train equipment in the back, taking me to all the places he needed and wanted to visit. I had some of the best times and conversations in my life in that car. He'd pick me up for an hour and I'd be gone all day. We talked all the way. He'd tell me about our ancestors, our family tree, what I came from. He'd tell me stories about his life, sometimes he'd ask about mine.

When he passed away, it was a soul-shattering blow to my heart. He was on a pedestal in my mind, and I had no desire to topple him down. And honestly, in my world, he deserved to be up there. It felt like a big seat was left sitting empty at the table in my heart. And I naturally looked to my partner at the time, someone I'd been in a serious relationship with for eighteen months, to take that seat for me. It wasn't a conversation that we had, more it was just an energetic change and shift in me towards him. For the first time in my womanly life, I needed a man to be something of a deep emotional support for me. I needed a king. Not a prince.

After having a necessary conversation with my partner at the time about what I meant to him, this partner of mine ghosted me and refused to see or speak with me ever again. It felt like two deaths in the space of one month. The man who had always been my king and the main man, and the man I thought was going to be that next, both gone just like that. I was crushed on more levels than I knew possible. On the surface he had shown up for me like a king but actually he turned out to be the biggest prince I had ever known. I literally went from waking to his good morning text or phone call every morning, seeing him most nights of the week, hearing from him at different times of the day, always getting a goodnight from him whether in person or on the phone, to nothing. Zilch. Nada. Nothing. Like I'd never existed to him or mattered. It was like someone had snuck up behind me and pulled the rug out from under my feet. I spent much of that year not knowing who I was grieving for.

A woman only has room for one king in her heart and mine had always been my grandad, and when I realised this, I realised something else. This meant I'd only ever had room for a prince to come sit down at the table in my heart. The king seat had already been taken in a very solid way. No one had ever really compared to my grandad in my eyes, and I'd deliberately chosen princes that could never have possibly filled or threatened his seat. Princes that didn't even want to.

If you're the apple of your father's eye or a daddy's girl, this might be why you've chosen princes for yourself too. This may even be stopping you from fully stepping into your highest self, your own version of a queen self. When I realised that I'd never wanted to topple my grandfather from his pedestal, I saw all the ways that my choices had kept him up there. My grandad was the safest source of love from a man in my life. Every princess needs a king to look after her and he was mine. I wish I'd learnt this before he passed. In many ways, my grandad passing was the invitation for me to become my own version of a queen and start my journey to becoming an energetic match to the now-empty king seat at my table. To step out of the princess seat I'd sat in so lovingly next to my grandfather, shuffle along the table and claim my new seat. And to then patiently keep living my life while I waited for someone to sit down in the empty seat beside me. If my grandad passing was the invitation to step into my queen seat and life path, my ex-partner ghosting me was the push. The following lessons after my grandad's passing were difficult because of the loss, but they have become increasingly graceful because of the personal gain. Before he passed, I talked about my sadness over this to him, that I could feel I was entering an exciting new beginning and season in my life but that he wasn't going to be here to witness it.

I feel a certain serendipity and a passing of the baton in the fact that the end of my grandad's life overlapped with a new beginning in mine. Within four weeks of his passing, everything that wasn't meant for me or good enough for me walked out of my life. From my career through to my love life. Everything I had thought was certain in my life, I discovered was not. I truly believe it was all of my grandfather's design. A woman only has room for one king in her life, just like a king only has room for one queen. Make sure you have your seats filled right.

32
HOW TO DROP INTO AND EMBRACE OUR FEMININE ENERGY

One of the hardest pills to swallow after leaving my marriage was realising just how much I'd been in my masculine energy during our relationship. I won't deny that he did cause some amount of it with his behaviour, but I did a beautiful job of perpetuating it also. I can see how I co-created our dynamic and enabled it to continue as it did. I can see how I added to our coming undone as a couple. Being in my masculine was definitely me in mum-energy to get everything done. It was also a self-protective mechanism I used to shield my heart from some of the more hurtful dynamics present in my marriage. I'm sharing this in case you've come to realise this too. Hindsight's a bitch sometimes when we see that life has left us with results that can't be undone quickly like we wish they could. This is a beautiful journey of learning along the way. Embrace that truth and be kind to yourself. There are no mistakes in life. Only lessons. Take the lessons always and run with them.

CREATE A LIFE THAT SUPPORTS THE FEMININE.

All of us have parts of our life that require us to operate from a driven, results-based and focused masculine space. Often this part of our life pays the bills and is our achieving side like our career. It can also be the energy that keeps the house going and ensures the children are at all of their after-school activities week to week. To prioritise the feminine, we need to bring more balance outside of those hours to support us in embracing and falling back into more of a feminine energy as often as we can. Cultivating and choosing to be in relationships that allow us to show up in our healthy feminine, warm, safe, intimate, where there is trust and respect is important here.

From my years of coaching women and from my personal experience, I can share that it is a challenge to be in our healthy feminine if our relationships are attacking, cruel, abusive or lacking in affection. In fact, if our relationships are abusive, it can sometimes be unsafe to be in our feminine energy more than our masculine. Adding more behaviours into our day, whether at the start, during our lunch break, or at the end of our day, that energetically move us back into our feminine is everything. This will move us from being in our head and place us back into our heart energy where a feminine woman mostly moves from.

Getting into the fresh air and sunshine, sitting with the peace of it all, journaling, free-flowing types of exercise like yoga or Pilates that energetically unwind us, freeform dance, and grounding our feet in the sand, grass or water are all wonderful practices. Literally anything that takes you out of your head and returns your attention into your heart space. Changing up how we dress outside of our careers can also be a great way to delineate between work self and feminine self, this might mean choosing softer colours, styles or cuts that speak to you in a feminine way outside of your nine to five.

BREATHE LIFE INTO YOUR FEMININE IN MOMENTS DURING THE DAY.

When we're too much in our head and acting from a place of thought, the feminine starts to feel drained, worn out, frayed and exhausted. This normally happens when we're in our masculine making decisions, analysing, planning, organising and over-thinking. A beautiful, discreet way to connect with our feminine during the day is to send our attention to the area in our womb space and disengage from our mind. I love to do this while walking. I focus my energy on that area and breathe down into my lower belly while softening my shoulders, heart and throat. You will find your walk will change slightly when you do this, your hips will soften and even take on a slight sway. Or if we're seated, we can simply take a moment to sit and breathe deeply while focusing our attention on the area in our womb space and disengaging from our mind. When you start playing with this practice, you will notice that men around you start to notice the shift in your energy! I experimented with this in the past with an ex-partner of mine. I found when I was in my head, he was less likely to touch me for no reason. But when I moved my focus to my womb space, I softened immediately and he responded, coming closer for no reason, touching for no reason. It was like a moth to a flame. He sought out my energy and warmth without realising he was. In your career and your everyday, taking moments like this will leave you feeling more connected and refreshed and, if you love the work that you do, purposeful.

Another beautiful and discreet way to bring subtle attention to your womb space in your day is to carry a yoni egg inside you. (Please seek advice from a professional therapist before use if you've never used a yoni egg before.) Explore this technique. You will be pleasantly surprised!

BEING VULNERABLE.

Vulnerability is not an invitation to air all of your dirty laundry or to post your every emotion on social media! Vulnerability isn't being needy. Vulnerability is sharing who we are with others, the real self underneath the façade and to show up freely as her. Being vulnerable is a necessary part of opening up to love, connection and passion. A healthy masculine energy has a natural desire to protect and provide for the feminine. He wants to feel the vulnerability and beauty deep inside of you. A woman who can embrace her own feminine energy, her own feminine strengths, will allow the space for a man to provide and care for her. And she will have more ease and joy in her relationships with men as a result. A woman who always has her everything-is-perfect façade on is not as deeply attractive to a healthy masculine man because he will feel unable to fully connect with her. One of the qualities healthy masculine men seek the most in an intimate relationship is that of a woman's warmth. Men are attracted to warm, friendly, open women they can relax with. This is different from easy or easy to please women. Very different, so please don't confuse the two.

Often women consider themselves warm and open when, in reality, they are only like that around their close friends. Whether you can be as freely yourself with a man as you are with your closest girlfriends is a beautiful barometer of where you are on this vulnerability scale. Are you the same person with your friends as you are with love interests? But please keep in mind here, not all men are deserving of this presence and energy from you. Steer yourself into a healthier feminine space and steer yourself towards healthy masculine men that know how to adore and appreciate you.

RELEASING THE NEED TO CONTROL THE OUTCOME.

There is a beautiful paradox in life that exists for all of us when we give up control, we in turn actually gain more freedom, power and relaxation on our path towards true happiness than we ever thought possible. I think of it as flowing with and seeing things as they are now over how we need them to be. Letting go and trusting the timing of life, trusting that others show up as best they know how when we leave them to their own devices, trusting that this approach creates space for true happiness in the long term, even if things don't evolve or eventuate as we wish, is a test for many of us to maintain. Our ego loves to feel a sense of control over the outcome. But it's an entirely false sense of control. Living with a sense of flow is accepting that we have no real control and that everything happens when it does and of its own accord. In love, this means if we want a man in our life who loves us, then we allow him the space to show us that he does. We don't step into the space and do the work for him. We give him both the space and the opportunity to do this himself. So many of us struggle with leaving this space because we're trying to control the outcome. We over-analyse, fall into anxiety, grow impatient and end up just doing it ourselves to close the space. Why do we do this? Often it is because of the feeling of uncertainty it brings to leave that space empty and waiting.

We tie up an awful lot of our self-worth, self-love and abandonment issues into that space and how quickly that space is closed. It's one of the biggest challenges I have with clients: to relax their need and compulsion to manipulate, cajole or bring about a certain result. Tony Robbins says it best, 'The quality of your life is in direct proportion to the amount of uncertainty you can comfortably deal with.'

Self-awareness and the ability to regulate ourselves in positive ways is everything here. As is understanding why we're doing this and to take a deep breath and distract ourselves before we do something to close the silence and the uncertainty. For me, embracing my feminine energy and choosing a life and relationship that supports living as this woman has completely opened up my world. It has changed my life. It has expanded me. I could never return to the woman I used to be; I could never tolerate or attract some of the things that I used to in my past relationships. I'm too soft and playful in my intimate relationships and too open a person for that now. I would never allow someone into my space who could ruin that energy in me now. This is the space I wish to see you in too. To find that curious, soft feminine energy within you, and to protect it like the queen you are.

33

EVERYTHING MAGIC THAT WILL HAPPEN TO YOU WILL OF ITS OWN MAGIC

We can't micromanage the universe. But gosh, sometimes like to try. Timing, outcomes, what someone is thinking, feeling—good luck trying to control any aspect of that. It is simply futile. I've learnt some beautiful life lessons about staying in the present and living with detachment to the outcome. On trusting the timing in my life, with hands wide open to the experience of life over hands tightly gripped onto people and things in an attempt to force them into being or staying a certain way. These lessons have cleared my energy and lightened the load that everyday living can sometimes place on our shoulders. And I wanted to share them with you.

LET YOUR LIFE UNRAVEL FORWARD IN FRONT OF YOU.

I don't hold on to what's no longer working or bringing me happiness. I believe this is a powerful technique in avoiding the mess because my hands are not clasped on to having anything remaining or staying a certain way. I try to always stay open. This means if it's not meant for me, there's no deep resistance from me. I let it go.

I FOLLOW THE BREADCRUMBS IN MY LIFE.

What's the obvious next step? Spirit signs. My intuition. The magic synchronicities and meant-to-bes that happen in life. I'm open to all of them speaking to me and take them as positive signs, breadcrumbs leading me to the path of my life. I follow them. This includes those times when my life path asks me to leave my comfort zone. Trust and have faith in the next step.

DON'T AVOID THE AVOIDABLE.

Usually, it's not hard to recognise when someone or something is no longer for us. It's just sometimes hard to accept. I don't choose to ignore what I want to ignore and see only what I want to see. I try to always witness things how they are.

IT'S IMPORTANT TO NOT PLACE MEANINGS ON THINGS, IT'S IMPORTANT TO STILL NOTICE THE SIGNS.

I try not to read between the lines or make assumptions. If it's an 'I don't know' or an 'I don't know why', I let it remain so until life shows me the answer. I don't try to close that space and uncertainty by creating a story for myself. I heal my anxiety over the lack of an answer with something else, like exercise or reading or catching up with friends. To me, this is living in flow and alignment with yourself and your life. This is flowing down stream rather than fighting to hold it together in one place, forcing things to happen at a certain time or in a certain way for you.

Maybe what is meant for you is better than what you've ever imagined happening for you. Why would we get in the way of that unfolding for us? There's a thought! If you pay attention to the patterns of your life and look back on the ones of the past, you'll realise that everything always works out. Everything always takes you to a greater destination next. You always grow, and the things you think you can't survive you somehow get through. That's the beauty of life. Always remember that. Tell me when leaving one thing didn't take you on to something else even more amazing and aligned for you next? Never! Your job is not to pave the path in front of you, but to keep facing your true north and to take one step forward after another on that path.

Things are not going to work out the way you are planning, how beautifully exciting. There are no shoulds, how freeing. Have faith and keep showing up because everything will work out even better than you could possibly imagine when you let go. Come what may. Stay what may. Believe me.

34

CHOOSING FROM YOUR WORTH OVER CHOOSING FROM YOUR WOUNDS

There's a big difference between choosing a relationship from our worth and choosing one from our wound. When we choose from our wound, we miss the red flags without realising we are. When we ignore our intuition, we self-abandon to maintain these relationships and ultimately seek out someone to heal us and love us as proof of us being good enough. Many of us are becoming more conscious about our choices and discerning about who and what we let into our hearts and bodies. Now is the time to become more self-aware than ever about this concept of wounds and begin to unravel and ask, what are mine?

Often, we continuously attract people into our life who represent healing for us. Healing that needs to happen through addressing unresolved lessons from our past, so we can move on. We're experiencing an unhealed wound from our past in the present moment when life or someone triggers us. It is essentially an open wound and subconsciously we are seeking out this next person who we hope will give us a new, happier ending and the healing our soul needs and seeks.

When we choose from our wounds, it looks like:
- Rushing into and defining a relationship based on honeymoon hormones.
- Choosing based on a fear of being alone.
- Wanting to be loved to feel 'good enough'.
- Feeling validated by someone having chosen us.

- Abandoning our needs to keep the peace and maintain the relationship by not acknowledging and following how we really feel or what we really desire from another.

When we choose from our worth, it looks like:
- Taking our time and not rushing.
- Qualifying our values: does this person move through life in a way that aligns with me and supports me?
- Asking: do we share common paths to build a relationship and life together that will celebrate us both?

Moving into a place of our highest self, where we feel the best we possibly can is truly the place where we can begin to draw higher levels of magic into our lives. In our relationships, our careers, pay cheque and friendships. In fact, our whole personal vibration lightens, lifts and brightens the more we are on our Queen Life Path, moving and choosing from a place of worth over our wounds. With every relationship you enter into in your future, I would love for you to ask yourself, is this relationship creating safety for my wounded self or is it a beautiful container for my highest self? Every relationship we choose for ourselves should ideally be one that holds us in our highest self-energy or one that inspires us to be in that energy more.

35
WHEN I LET PEOPLE LOVE ME, THEY

When I let people love me, they… What was the first word or full answer that came to mind for you? The first answer that comes immediately to mind is almost always the right one. Our answer to this question says so much about our beliefs, expectations and conditioning around love. This is a representation of a core wound we need to heal and move you through.

>   When I let people love me, they … *leave me.*
>   Why do you believe this?
>   Who was the first person to really leave you?

>   When I let people love me, they … *hurt me.*
>   Why do you believe this?
>   Who was the first person who taught you to love someone, meant you would be hurt?

There are many varied answers to this question: use me, take advantage of me, lie to me, betray me, think they own me. Our answer simply highlights our past experiences with love. And unless your answer is something along the lines of when I let people love me, they love and adore me, then it's something we need to heal and explore. For as long as we believe something, we will manifest it. Our beliefs are self-perpetuating, and through our choices we validate our perception of the world. Change these and we change our results.

>   When I let people love me, they love me back.
>   When I let people love me, they love and adore me.

When I let people love me, they can't help but fall in love with me. When I let people love me, they stay.

Whichever resonates for you (or a version of your own, of course), she deserves to be written on your bathroom mirror in red lipstick for a time until you feel it in your body to be true and meant for you.

36
HOW TO KNOW WHAT YOU ARE VIBRATIONALLY ALIGNED FOR

I've learnt there's what we say we desire and there's where we actually spend all of our time, attention, thought. There's what we say is important to us and there's what we actually think about, desire, crave. This so often explains the phenomenon of what we say we want not showing up for us. It is our often our subconscious mind, rather than our conscious thought that presents us with results in our life. We say we want love, but the majority of our focus is on our careers and financial independence. So, our careers blossom. We say to ourselves that our career is important to us, but actually our eye is looking for love, connection and laughter. So, forms of love show up. There is no right or wrong. There is just the season that you're in and whether it's aligned with what it is you truly want.

Where focus goes, results flow. Sometimes we just have to honour the season we really are in, knowing it's not going forever but it is where I need to be right now, and throw ourselves into it with full attention and excitement. It's often so beautiful what shows up for us when we're happily focused on the season, we're truly in. The magic of serendipity, where what's meant for us arrives in our life of its own magic and accord.

37

WOMEN, STOP YOUR HUNTING, YOU'RE NOT GOOD AT IT

He's not for everyone but I love some of Steve Harvey's work and his thoughts on dating and the dynamic between men and women. It does align with how I choose to move through the world. It doesn't have to for you. I believe his approach also aligns with the innate biology of men and women and with the divine masculine and feminine energies. In his words, 'Women, take yourself out of the hunting business because it's not what you do. Men are hunters. We hunt all day. That's what we do. Stop your hunting. You're not good at it.' In my own personal and professional experience, I have found this to be almost always true. When a man knows what he wants, he will make himself known to you. He might do it in a loud, more pronounced way, or he might do it in a mild-mannered way. Either way, he will make himself known to you, he will put himself in your path in some way.

I believe it's not a woman's job to hunt down men. It's my experience that when we do, we end up inadvertently hunting the wrong kind of men for us. Often the one we regret having ever met. I know this chapter might sound entirely politically incorrect in a world where women are rightly given much the same opportunities as men. But most of us have experienced this at one time or another, when a man knows what he wants he rarely hesitates long to try and capture it. In fact, he will often go out of his way to make it happen. And let's be honest with ourselves, ladies. When a man is like this does, it is next-level. I only want a man who knows what he wants. I have no desire to capture a man and convince him that he wants me. I believe every woman should love with this energy. In every consensual, reciprocal, romantic exchange I've had with a man, if I've felt him hunting me and I've decided I like the look and energy of him, then I've slowed down just enough to let him know that I was open to his hunting and made it just that little, little bit easier for him to start a conversation with me. Whatever that first interaction might have been.

For women, this is true. We very subtly help out the guy we like. When I date, I keep that same energy. A man hasn't captured us just because we said yes to talking to him or going on a date with him. For me, I'm still weighing him up and deciding if I like him, the decision isn't his.

I see and coach too many women that fall for someone simply because he chose them and gave them attention. No! It's not about that. What about how much you really like him? What about if he's good enough for you or not? So, if it's more of the man's role to be the hunter, where does it leave us? To stand there and look pretty? Waiting like prey? No. It's to be on our Queen Life Path. To be happy and content in ourselves, wrapped up in doing our own thing, open for love when it comes, looking and feeling good and enjoying our own life in the best possible way. It is a man's job to place himself on our path and keep himself there. Not our job to drag him onto it and hold him there. Men do value what they need to chase and work for a little. I'm not at all telling you to be manipulative or play games. I am suggesting that you let him put in the thought and effort to plan. And it's for you to not merge your energy with his so early, just because he's given you some attention, you don't know enough about him yet.

Dismiss this chapter entirely if it doesn't align with your beliefs, but I'm a big believer in this approach.

38

JUST NOT THAT INTO YOU, WHY LOW-EFFORT MEN TRIGGER A TRY HARDER RESPONSE

There are many labels out there for men in the dating world right now: narcissistic, toxic, emotionally unavailable. But if we dig deep further, what we might also see are our own ego tricks here. Our ego doing its best to keep us safe from rejection and perceived criticism by making it about them and not us. I know that this can initially make us feel a little defensive, but stay with me, please!

I'm going to make a broad generalisation, but there are generally two types of men out there in the dating world. The first is the man who is excited to meet the one. He's ready. This man is always honest and upfront about what he's looking for. He doesn't hesitate to show a woman who he is interested in or what he thinks and feels about her. These men are sure about what they want. The second type of man is still focused on building (or rebuilding) his career, his life, his financial standing, and isn't looking to invite a queen into his castle just yet. He isn't looking for that distraction. This guy is almost always honest and upfront about his needs from the start too. In his words and in his behaviour. He may fall in love with a woman during this time, yes. But only if he meets a true match and feels that this woman can contribute to building his castle. And if this happens, then he won't hesitate to show her how he thinks and feels about her. How often do women encounter this second type of man, and instead of taking him at his words or actions, fall into thinking they can change his mind or change how he feels about them. I see women do this all the time. All the time. So, what I'm asking you is to consider if he really is emotionally unavailable, looking for a relationship or maybe just not that into you? If we hadn't put as much effort and time into these relationships, would some of them have lasted as long as they did? Some might not have even really started or got off the ground if we hadn't made ourselves so available. Something for us to ponder on as women is the ways in which we enabled the relationship to persist even though it didn't truly meet all of our needs.

I'm yet to meet anyone who doesn't come with some degree of baggage. Me included. Even after years of self-work and reflection and journeying through all of it, I still have baggage. We all have our triggers. I do believe that as women need to stop alienating and criticising the masculine as much as we do. We do ourselves and them no favours. One sex is not more evolved or better than the other. Just because men don't communicate or move through the world like we think they should, that doesn't make us right, it just makes us different. Many labels we project onto men to explain away their treatment or rejection of us are just that. Projections. Projections that might be protecting us from fully having to sit with truths that hurt to admit, our own role in things unfolding as they did.

I'm not making excuses for men here at all. Ghosting, disappearing, pulling away and not communicating emotions is immature and uncaring behaviour. But I'm going to elaborate for you. Men are simple. We like to make men out to be more complicated than they are because as women we like to talk, and this veers so very easily into talking too much about ourselves, analysing our life and relationships to the point of creating stories and assumptions about the situation. Ones that often don't quite match the reality. Men are simple. Low effort is low effort. And if low effort is triggering an 'I need to try harder' response from you, then I'm going to come right out and say something. This tells me that first and foremost, you are probably not owning or understanding your own value or worth. Effort needs to increase as the relationship evolves, not decrease, a simple truth we often forget when someone has hooked us in but then only gives us enough to keep us there. We don't have to earn effort or work for it. But sometimes, for some reason, we seem to like to. As though working for it somehow means he likes us more. Actually, it's the opposite. The less we have to work for his attention, the more he actually likes us. Read that sentence again, please, if you need to.

Low-effort behaviour actually triggers in us two wounded responses that make us feel we need to try harder to capture their love and attention. Continuing to chase and pursue a man even though his behaviour makes us feel terrible about ourselves is a classic form of self-abandonment. You, my dear, are worth all the effort and then some. And I'm going to remind you again, because it's so important and clear a sentence. The less we have to work for his love and attention, the more he actually likes us. No one needs to work that hard to be loved. Certainly not you.

39
FUTURE TRIPPING AND HOW WE SOMETIMES CREATE OUR OWN PAIN

Ladies. Can we please acknowledge that sometimes we cause much of our own pain when we go future tripping on ourselves. Whether we've gone from first date in real life to marrying him in our head because he is so perfect, and the date went so well to holding on to what may now be an outdated dream, where it started off so well between you both and now, you're holding on, hoping it will get back to how it was. Releasing imagined futures and our need for them is one of the hugest clarifiers you will ever have in your relationships. All of a sudden, how someone is rather than how we want them to be now becomes vastly apparent. Let your man show up beautifully for you in the now or not if he's not doing that. Yes, everyone has potential. But can we just acknowledge how hard it is to inspire and motivate ourselves to change and show up for ourselves? How impossible it is to try to inspire someone else! Particularly if they're not open or ready.

Release your imagined future and story. It's all make-believe. Instead consider if you are enjoying time with him now. Does the now feel delicious and fun and giving between you both? Is he showing you that he's interested? Is he bringing out the best in you? And stay always on your own Queen Life Path, focusing only on your next few steps ahead. If he's meant to be in your future, let him be, but don't go writing the script out for him just yet.

40

BE PATIENT, MIRACLES TAKE LONGER THAN SETTLING DOES

If you think you're settling, you almost always are. Finding peace on the journey has been one of my biggest life lessons since leaving my marriage. I was always so results focused. So impatient. And it really took away from me being able to enjoy the process and the evolving of my life. My desire to be somewhere other than where I was, for something to be more than it was, often led to me settling. At the time, I felt it was better to have something than to have nothing. When we stop settling is when we can truly call in what we deserve. In fact, every time we settle, it reinforces that little part inside of us that wonders if we're good enough. You are capable of calling in more. Just because you haven't experienced the ease, love and life you wish for in the past doesn't mean it won't exist for you in the future. There is no need for anyone in life to settle for anything less than what they deserve and what lights them up.

Timing is everything. Magic is real. Be patient. The serendipitous nature of our lives is truly beautiful when we allow and believe in this energy of what is meant for us always finding us. Leave the space open for everything you truly want and deserve. Live your life path happily until what's meant for you presents itself. It's on its way. I know it's going to look so different for you than you could ever expect now. And I know that when you reach that person and space, you wouldn't wish it to have happened any other way. Keep going. And enjoy the many pots of gold you're going to discover along the way.

Part Two

The Queen Path, Moving on in Love After a Divorce

41
THERE ARE NO WRONG PARTNERS

I write this knowing that it is easier to accept for those who chose or who are the ones choosing to end their marriages. A much more bitter pill to swallow for those who feel abandoned, mistreated or left behind. However, we shouldn't have nor hold any bitterness because the lessons remain the same, there are no wrong partners. No wasted years. They were precisely the person you needed for the stage of evolution that you were at when you met. Who you attracted and ended up marrying helped reveal to you your limiting beliefs which allowed you the opportunity to transcend them. This is as true for you as it was for your partner. Maybe you transcended your limiting beliefs or maybe they did. Typically, the one who transcended their limiting belief is the one who chose to end the relationship. Almost everyone comes to their first marriage believing they needed it for reasons outside of themselves. This is typically a reflection of us having chosen a partner and having entered a relationship at an age where we barely knew ourselves and hardly understood our future needs and potential.

The stereotypes that I see so often here will ring true for many. Men who thought it was time for them to settle down and be responsible. They'd been single long enough, played the field for long enough so they chose to marry the woman who ticked all the boxes. Or she fell pregnant to him, so they married, which was the responsible, right thing to do. Only to find themselves emotionally and sexually disconnected and somewhat bored years later because he made the stability, security, sensible, right choice. These men typically end up with everything that was once their version of success on paper, the house, the family, the career, the money, but it lacks what their soul really desires: passion and a deep, loving connection. Women who chose their partners because they were confident with money, successful and good providers. Men who knew where they were going in life which ultimately saved her from having to step into these qualities for herself. She goes on to leave her husband because in time she begins to feel too controlled, repressed, manipulated and unappreciated. He is structured and controlling, and now she seeks freedom and wants to grow. After years of accepting less than loving behaviour from her partner and staying because she was fearful about providing for herself financially, she eventually reaches a point of 'I can't do this anymore, I'm done.'

Relationships are often chosen because of a void within us. For example, a person will give me what I don't have in myself, or they will save me from this or that. It's an attempt to skip the necessary self-growth that eventually catches up with us later in life. The ending of love and relationships can take on a completely new level if we view them from this perspective. However, the lesson can be still hard to accept. A soul entered your life at one point of your evolution where you were perhaps out of balance within yourself, until yours or their evolution outgrew the necessity for the other in the relationship.

If someone left you, however they chose to do it, it's because their soul outgrew you and your dynamic as a couple. If you left someone, it's because your soul outgrew them and your dynamics as a couple. This is a bitter pill to swallow for some, that your time with someone ended if you weren't ready for it to end or didn't feel the same way. Will we reach a point of soul evolution where we will not outgrow another? Yes, I believe that we do. More about that later.

42

WHY ARE SO MANY JADED ABOUT LOVE AND MARRIAGE

How many marriages or relationships that exist in your social or familial world around you would you want to have for yourself? Think on this for a moment. When I ask my clients this, I always hear a shade of the same answer, only a few, or one or two. If we sit with this mind-blowingly low result, what is it telling us? Not that love doesn't exist or that marriages are hard work that require large amounts of self-sacrifice and compromise; it's a reflection of couples staying in relationships and marriages where they are no longer in love or feel happy or that they've outgrown but family, obligation and marriage have kept them tied together. It's a reflection that so many love relationships today are going around in a cycle of repeated patterns and behaviours, compounded over time by many years of biting tongues, keeping the peace and the occasional argument when it all gets too much. A cycle that has repeated itself enough over time to slowly kill the emotional connection, deep intimacy and love. It's also a reflection of how well so many of us see through the personalities and intricacies that others think they're presenting so well to the world. And we wonder why so many of us are jaded about love and marriage. The result is couples and individuals who have not let go of relationships that they probably should have released years ago.

Look at what surrounds us. Look what we are modelling to our next generation. Consider what was modelled to us. There is so little representation of what a truly loving, healthy, happy relationship looks like in most of our worlds. Instead, we are surrounded by a lot of settling, mediocrity, holding on and varying degrees of self-abandonment and tolerating in the name of marriage. This is not where I want to hear you say it's easier to stay single. This is where I want you to start waking up to the realisation that you having left your marriage means that you now get to be in and create the example for your children and for others that you didn't have represented to yourself.

Some people meet the one that they connect with emotionally, sexually and intimately in a deep way early in life. They grow together and their relationship deepens in all the ways as they deepen as a couple. To meet this person early in life is like winning the jackpot. It doesn't happen for all of us. The truth is that most of us weren't of the energetic match capable of being in such a relationship so early in life. This is why many of us meet this person later in life. We weren't ready for them to be in our lives any earlier. We wouldn't have known what to do with such a love and we certainly wouldn't have appreciated it. It's why we often marry and procreate with one person early in life when we are at the prime age to do so but go on to meet our forever one with someone else later in life. We have, through life and experience, evolved enough in our souls to be ready and prepared for such a love.

I wish more married couples who are dissatisfied and sticking it out realised this. Sometimes the most powerful and conscious thing we can do is to let go of a love that at one time was a match for our evolution but now is not. Many of you reading this will resonate with that sentiment. It might just be slower or harder for you to accept if you are the one who has been left and are feeling abandoned or hurt as a result. To accept that your ex-partner saw this writing on the wall before you did or at least wanted to do something to resolve it before you did or saw the need.

43

WHAT HAPPILY MARRIED COUPLES TELL ME

I've had many professional success stories of clients who have gone on to find the most amazing partners for themselves after divorce. In my own life, I've also had some beautiful examples of couples who were still genuinely happy after many years of marriage to watch and reflect on. It might surprise you to hear what they think and have told me. They look at unhappy, disconnected, grown apart couples and they wonder how and why they're still doing it to themselves. I also hear this same sentiment from many clients of mine who are divorced when they look at these married couples. Why are they still there doing that to themselves? I could never go back to that. Once a person feels happiness, joy and a sense of freedom and appreciation to be all of themselves in life without criticism or constraint. Once they taste how that feels and they are loved for it, that becomes their new normal. They don't want to lose that feeling.

Sometimes we don't realise what we were settling for and tolerating to keep a relationship together until we are out of it. Time is always the biggest indicator of relationship dynamics that we came to accept as normal, only to realise after we leave and as we move onto our next love that they weren't necessarily healthy dynamics at all; it was simply all that we'd ever really known.

44
WHAT I THINK ABOUT MANY MARRIAGES

Unhappy, disconnected or unsatisfying marriages inhibit the evolution of a soul. So do relationships that we've outgrown but are staying in for reasons like children, finances or convenience. I'm not talking about the dynamic of the family unit here. Family and marriage are separate entities. I'm talking about the dynamic of two individuals within a couple.

You wouldn't believe the things that I hear. The things that individuals have tolerated, settled for or believed about themselves to keep their marriage going and together are the absolute rubbish that some people have put up with in the name of marriage and staying married. And people still feel guilty and a sense of failure for wanting to leave or a deep sadness for someone having left them after treating them miserably for years. Affairs and cheating. Sometimes repeatedly over years. Emotional abuse and manipulation. Financial and emotional control. Purposefully belittling their partners. Lying. Horrible, repeated name calling and mind games. Gaslighting. The slow slippery slope where we bite our tongues and keep the peace over little things in the early stages of our marriages that are not a big deal. Only to find ourselves keeping the peace over things much larger many years down the path. Behaviour that at the beginning we would have never tolerated or accepted. Behaviour we would never have imagined we would end up having to tolerate in time. This, all in the name of marriage and keeping a marriage together. This slow, slippery slope.

I understand it, I truly do. It was my own personal journey over many years that cost me my confidence, self-worth and self-esteem.

A path that took years to rebuild because so much of what I was tolerating crept into my psyche. It was one of the most humbling things I had to accept after my marriage ended. Just how negative staying in my marriage had been for me over the cumulative years I was in it. Even though I thought I'd done a strong and wonderful job of not letting some of the negative dynamics affect my sense of self, over time they had.

I am not anti-marriage or pro-marriage. I am pro adults being in loving relationships with partners who love and accept them beautifully for all of who they are. Moreso, I am pro individuals being in relationships that bring out and celebrate the best in them. For me, the question is never about marriage and whether it is a good or bad institution. It is about love and the quality of love that exists between the couple.

Seeing through the façade of successful lives and social constructs like marriage is my profession. In my profession I am allowed to glimpse behind the façade of both through talking with my clients in our private sessions. They can share with me, without restrictions, what's really going on in their minds, their relationships and what's not going on in their bedrooms. I've heard it all. And I hear it all without judgement. Many of my clients are the villains for ending their marriages in the way they have, or they are the victims of someone having ended their marriage cruelly. Working in this space has changed my values and perceptions entirely about humans and what we strive for and value.

I no longer desire the things I used to desire because I see and hear how unhappy, trapped and miserable so many people truly are with all those values that many of us once bought into and deemed as success. It's lost all of its gloss to me as I'm sure it has for some of you here. The beautiful home. Happy family life. The obligation to keep it all together because they've worked so hard for it and sacrificed so much, because they're viewed in such a way for having what they have.

The institution of marriage is heralded as this wonderful thing that we must perpetuate to uphold the values of society. The values become the trap. That's not love. That's marriage. We weren't born to one day get married and forever stay married, happily or not. We were born to love, to expand and to grow as a soul and enjoy a life experience defined by love.

My soul would choose love and that experience over marriage any day. Even if that means having to leave a marriage to be able to find that love and experience again with another. And actually, I choose it for you too because I know everything that it will lead you to in time. Even if you don't feel this way in this moment. A more expansive life. A more expansive soul. A more expansive love.

45
WHY ARE WE SEEING MORE DIVORCES NOW THAN EVER

There is a lot of discussion around the throwaway culture many perceive exists around relationships and marriages that end today, as though people are no longer trying as hard as they did in previous generations (or as much as they should). There is talk that as a society we no longer value family and commitment like we once did. My professional experience is that for the majority of individuals, this is an unfair narrative. Very few leave a marriage without deliberating over their decision and the consequences for everyone involved for a considerable period of time first. This is often an internal process, sometimes for years, before it is expressed outwardly. What might seem like an out-of-the-blue decision was often far from sudden in someone's head. In fact, statistically, we know that many individuals stay in a marriage for twelve to eighteen months longer than they perhaps should have and for every reason that they're later criticised and accused of not caring about family, the children, everything they've built together. Before they leave, these individuals sit with a lot of turmoil, self-doubt, guilt, shame and fear for wanting to leave or for having left. Even more so how their loved ones will react and deal with a separation.

I meet very few individuals who have not deliberated silently for a lengthy period of time about what to do, often for years before they discuss with their partners about their intention to separate or that they felt the relationship was over which tends to sadly come as a complete surprise to them. So why are people leaving marriages and asking for a divorce more now than ever before? Simply put, because they can. In previous generations they either couldn't or at least felt they couldn't. Trying to compare divorce statistics now with those from previous generations is like trying to compare apples and oranges: two different periods of time with two different kinds of societal structures existing around them. This is why we are currently seeing an increase in divorces particularly in the Generation X (individuals born mid-60s to 80s) and Baby Boomers (individuals born between 1946 to 1964). In my opinion, it is a flushing of the pond of relationships that perhaps should have ended earlier but didn't because society frowned upon it more then. These marriages consist of individuals who had outgrown their partners in many ways but who stayed for reasons like family, fear, finances or responsibility.

This also looks like individuals who came from parents who had divorced or who had unhappy marriages. They desired to create a home life and relationship for themselves and their children that was the complete antithesis of their parent's relationship and childhood experience. However, they then find themselves having created a wonderful family unit but alongside an empty, disconnected and sometimes unsatisfying relationship.

While it might be true that they passed down to their children an improved childhood experience, that over emphasis on family and children didn't facilitate the loving relationship that they necessarily imagined for themselves. Divorce just wasn't seen as an option in the past like it is today. It wasn't as socially accepted and therefore happened rarely. Someone really had to be suffering terribly within their marriage for it to be socially justifiable to leave, domestic violence, persistent adultery, and behaviours sadly associated with addictions. But even then, many women and men often stayed in these marriages because of the stigma of divorce but also the lack of support and financial capability to do so. Therefore, the narrative had to become that family comes first, family is everything and staying together for the children is the responsible and best parenting choice.

Individuals, especially women, had no real choice to model anything else differently even if they desired too. Staying married and keeping the family together became the sole focus and the suburban dream and version of success. It was the belief that being in a marriage, for better, for mediocre, or for worse was what we should first aspire to. And everything in life outside of that was to be built up around it.

This works perfectly of course if the marriage is built on a strong foundation of love, connection and intimacy that continues to exist throughout the marriage. It works less perfectly if that foundation changes or gains many cracks over time to the point of barely being held together. Like a house of cards, marriages like that will always, in time, fall down. Now and in future generations. In many ways it is a different level of human consciousness and awareness today than was lived in previous generations. The husband went to work all day. He earnt the money and provided for the family. That was his job done. He came home to a cooked dinner. Spent some time with the family, if at all. His emotional contribution was often very little. The wife's role was to stay home and care for the children. Her emotional contribution was everything to the family unit. All of this with the occasional holiday thrown in. It was the accepted system and social matrix of behaviour that many of our parents followed and, as a result, many of us also followed without much thought given. First, we do this, and then we do that, and then this, and then win, we are successfully adulting.

Personal happiness, personal growth or personal fulfillment really didn't form a central point of anyone's thoughts or conversation.

Back then, society really didn't support personal growth or soul evolvement. Quality of life is determined not just by our financial status and lifestyle anymore. As adults now, personal growth, happiness and soul evolvement are what many of us prioritise and desire. Even if they don't use those words and recognise that this is what they're really seeking, for a life and love that feels as good on the inside as it looks on the outside. One that is true, authentic and aligned with who we are. The manner in which the level of human consciousness has now grown and evolved is because it has the capacity to do so.

For security, stability and safety. We have to remember that up until and throughout the 1970s, The Marriage Bar required women to give up their jobs once they were married and women were not allowed to get a mortgage without needing a male guarantor. In many ways, women did not have the same rights or opportunities as men. This woman threw herself into her children and built a beautiful home. She lived and looked the part. She identified with this role. And she sat with her friends, and they moaned and gossiped about their husbands to one another and what they were doing or not doing over cups of tea and coffee to socially connect. She hoped to not come out feeling like the worse off woman in the room which justified why she was staying in her own marriage but also gave her something to talk about with her husband 'can you believe so and so is doing this...'

It would be naïve of us to not consider that all of these social structures, restrictions and beliefs were not created purposefully to keep adults in social order and that the trauma and fear of restrictions and beliefs of previous generations haven't been handed down to both sexes as learnt behaviour. All of this keeps men and women in a cycle of woundedness and co-dependency, unable to stand in their own power, their own brilliance and in their full confidence alongside and in love with another human being in their own power, brilliance and full confidence, all because social structures and conditioning didn't support or allow them to leave.

It is a very different energy. Two humans at their best. Equals. Choosing to be together. Not stuck with one another. In love. Choosing to be with one another. A very different energy than is found in most marriages today. This is something I have no qualms in saying despite the controversy it might bring because of the number of conversations I have with so many individuals about what is really happening in their lives and marriages. Women may fear the financial, familial and social consequences of change if they were to leave but they now have more opportunity than ever to be financially independent and strong and to carve their own lives without having a male partner at the centre. It is often the belief in their own capabilities that they lack and a lack of awareness and education to know what to do next now that they are making all the big life decisions on their own. Yet, if women look around today, they can see more and more women thriving in their lives post-divorce.

Men may worry about the financial consequences of change and the fallout it might cause in some of their relationships with friends and family if they were to leave, but they are growing more and more in their emotional awareness than previous generations. More present and involved fathers. Better connected socially with family and friends. And being that most men were typically the main provider for the family, their earning potential and ability to thrive financially into the future often remains unchanged. It is often the fear that their role as a father in the eyes of their children may diminish or change if the marriage was to end. That their standing within the family may be tarnished. Yet, if men look around now, they can see more and more men thriving in this space post-divorce and with their relationships with their children still intact, loving and connected.

Yes, divorce is only happening now more than ever because it can. Not because we care less about love or relationships or need them any less. Not because we don't value marriage but because we desire to be married to someone that genuinely loves and cares for us on an intimate level. All certainty that someone must stay with you forever has been removed from marriage now. There are no guarantees. An individual has to want to and desire to stay with an individual. No one is beholden to another.

Many are not happy to see this forever safety, security and certainty around marriage start to slacken and disappear. I hear from these individuals in my emails and my social media DMs, many disgusted with the work that I do in this space and the way I support people to leave unhappy marriages. I am, they say, encouraging divorce. The truth these individuals in my inbox are ignoring on a soul level. There is no certainty in love and no guarantee that someone will continue to love you and feel the same way for you. And there never has been.

There was only ever certainty in marriage and marriage is a social construct we created as humans. Marriage for those who feel disconnected, dissatisfied, abused, taken for granted, or who have grown out of love with their partner is not a wonderous construct. It is a trap. One they wish they could slide out of. And someone who is staying in a marriage because it feels right or responsible. Or because they want to keep their financial assets, home and lifestyle together is not contributing to the growth and evolvement of our society. They are actually contributing to the social order that marriage creates. The social order that is keeping them trapped. No wonder the journey to finding love after divorce is such a different one. We are moving against the social order that many around us are still in happily or not for either reasons of love or safety or security. We so often have to upset and disappoint so many that we love on the pathway to choosing ourselves, our happiness and having the courage to voice it.

Love after divorce is a different kind of love entirely. And it will require a more evolved, better version of self if we hope to do it successfully. Otherwise, we will only go on to repeat our past patterns and conditioning.

46
I WANT YOU TO START SEEING THIS PERSPECTIVE

(IF YOU DON'T ALREADY)

I'd love for you to sit with this. Imagine what kind of world we would be living in if the majority of adults, instead of the minority, were in a relationship that was loving, passionate, connected, healthy, fulfilling—one that celebrated the best in both people. Beautifully loved up couples everywhere. Living life as their best selves. Imagine the flow-on effect into the world of witnessing this kind of love and its impact on our children who live and learn vicariously through us. I want you to start seeing the limitedness, inertia and heaviness associated with so many marriages around you, if you don't already. Not because marriage is an outdated or negative institution, but because there are too many couples still married when they perhaps shouldn't be. Envisage what this is contributing to our society, our children, our values and our collective evolution.

I want you to begin imagining this. Imagine if the majority of adults had a full emotional and energetic scope to completely focus on all of the outside elements of their life and self because the love relationship of their life was easeful, balanced, caring, loving and allowed them the energetic space to do so. There was no drama or unfulfilling relationship dynamic worrying them or clouding their thoughts, essentially sapping their energy on a daily basis. No home scenario or relationship they had to manage. Nobody ghosting them, lying to them, manipulating them. No disconnection emotionally or physically. No negative emotions or thoughts they had to manage or rise above regarding their relationship situation.

Imagine what each individual could potentially create in their own life if they were free from the weight of all of this. Society would be of a very different energy. Adults awake and awakening into the fullest expressions of themselves. Thriving and loved up. Creative even. And free to be so. Begin to imagine that.

47

WHAT DOES IT REALLY MEAN WHEN WE LEAVE A MARRIAGE

Leaving a marriage is us breaking through our conditioning and our fears. Someone leaving us forces us to breakthrough by consequence not by choice. The marriage we chose for ourselves when we were in our twenties and thirties is the one that family and social circles shaped us to choose. This is called conditioning. This relationship is typically a soulmate relationship. One that many outgrow as a result. What I am starting to say more often to my clients is this: most couples who remain only in this relationship for life are potentially, more than likely, hindering their soul growth. A common misconception of soulmates that we will explore later in this book is that they are our 'one'. Usually, they are not. It's why our own divorce can not only trigger us to feel fear and uncertainty but also trigger those around us too. Our behaviour is going against the expected norm and social order. We are choosing different for ourselves. And we are no longer choosing to tolerate what many around us are still choosing to tolerate and buy into.

Not everyone is comfortable with having their perceptions of relationships threatened. It's why many people can feel selfish, guilt or shame for wanting to end a marriage. It's why those who have been left can feel abandoned and more alone than ever before. The loss of the safety blanket of having a someone or being a someone for another, whether they treat us well or not, can be painful. We are very much breaking away from the pack and choosing ourselves when we leave a marriage. Sometimes for the very first time. It's why people-pleasing behaviour can be so often associated with marriages. When we are a people-pleaser, we put our needs last, even at the expense of our health, wellbeing or sense of self. Abandoning our needs like this is often linked to our self-worth and our fear of losing love and our place within the tribe of family. People-pleasing is entrenched in a desire to belong at whatever personal cost. Choose to not see what is really happening in front of us. We keep the peace at the abandonment and detriment of ourselves until the personal cost becomes too much, too hard to ignore or distract ourselves from. Or our more grown-up children look to us one day and let us know that they can see you are not happy, asking why are you still there, giving us permission to leave. Removing the risk and fear we'd been carrying of leaving a marriage that might potentially have cost us a relationship with our children. When someone leaves a marriage, it is because either the dissatisfaction or consequences of continuing to stay in the marriage wakes them up. Or the arrival of someone else into their life and heart has woken them up to what they now need in a lover and partner.

In life, humans are either moving forward and making decisions to avoid pain or they are moving forward and making decisions towards pleasure. What many don't realise is that it's not our human-ness that chooses to leave a marriage. It is our soul that is calling out for more, for better, for freedom. It is the soul's discontent with the world. When we leave a marriage, we are choosing to listen to and move forward with our soul over the voice of our mind though often not even realising that we are. A marriage ending is a soul wake-up call.

It's why the love journey after divorce is so different. You are different by consequence from having left a marriage and from having to walk away from the conditioning that you once bought into and believed was the dream. This is the same dream that those are around you and still married are still buying into or at least pretending to behave like they do so they don't lose everything. A choice was made from the point of someone's soul when a marriage ended, that their personal happiness mattered more to them than everyone else's happiness, expectations or responsibilities placed upon them. They've made the choice that their personal happiness matters more than the money, the home they love or the lifestyle they enjoy. And the personal choice we make now once we leave a marriage is to either continue living from the point of our soul or to fall back into the trap of leading from our humanness, choosing what society deems is sensible for us, choosing from a place of ego or from how we like to be seen or viewed by others. Choosing from a place of wound or from a place of worth. We either awaken further or we fall back to sleep.

48

A LOVE NOTE TO MEN AND WOMEN BEFORE WE GO ANY FURTHER TOGETHER

I hear these two sentiments from men and women all the time. Where are all the good men in the world? Where are all the good women in the world?

Let's talk about why both sexes feel jaded by the other. It surprises many women to hear this, but many men do want to meet the right woman. To be happy, live in peace, enjoy the simple things and have amazing sex until the sun goes down. They don't want to settle and take on what feels like drama as much as women don't want to settle or take on drama. And many men are not interested in having casual sex as much as some women think. For many men, it's lost its appeal because it attracts a certain type of woman which brings stress and a certain level of crazy into their lives (their words, don't shoot the messenger!). Many men consider relationships to be hard work, so they don't enter them lightly.

Women, knowing that it is the men's turn next, I'd love for you to please hold any inner rebukes you may have about men knowing it's important to equally hear from them too. While yes, many men may be adept at dodging blame. Professionally, I'd love to share with you that, in my experience, many women are well-skilled at projecting onto others. Women can be well-practised at shutting a man down and for making him feel bad for having said the wrong thing. Which is why men shy away from saying the truth and tell you what they think they need or want to hear, they don't want to hurt or disappoint you. They don't want to fight. In fact, many have no idea about what to do with your emotions, so they do their best to avoid them.

Not all women reading the above paragraph are going to agree with my sentiment. But it is what men tell me all the time. A man's perspective is different because it is allowed to be, and they are wired in a completely different way to women. And if I can ask one thing in the defence of men today, it is for women to stop assuming or seeing men as being less evolved or less emotionally in tune as women. This is an unfair narrative I see many women hold and it is not a true reflection of all men. Men are entirely different creatures than women and many are trying more than you know. Many men are struggling emotionally more than they feel safe to communicate. All I ask is that we let them be who they are without criticism or looking down on them. I am always going to be an advocate for having more strong men at their best and in their power in the world today as much as I am women. We need more of both. I write this knowing that both sexes are unwittingly going to disappoint others and hurt others on the pathway to becoming this, their behaviour being the reason why you hold the view that you do.

What I hear from men:
- So many women are anxious and needy.
- It's so easy to manipulate women because they need attention and to be loved so much.
- Women expect us to look like something out of a magazine with a six-pack. She doesn't even have one.
- Everyone wants a guy who is financially secure or successful. I don't want a dependant or someone who needs saving.
- So many women out there are nutty.
- There is more peace in my life when I'm not in a relationship.
- I don't know if I want to be in a relationship again because I end up losing all of my freedoms and feel controlled.

Many women don't trust men and view them with quite a large degree of caution. They feel manipulated and misused. Taken for granted. More and more women are choosing to be single and stay single because the hurt that men have caused them has been traumatic. They are tired of the dating cycle and going through so many lousy, disappointing, manipulative men. They are focusing on themselves. They are throwing themselves into their careers. They are opting out of casual dating and choosing to hold out until they meet a guy who knows how to love them right.

What I hear from women:
- Men don't know what they want.
- I don't want another man-child who needs saving.
- Men are more interested in how a woman looks and her youth than what is on the inside. I feel overlooked and like I don't matter anymore.
- I look around and regularly don't feel good enough.
- Men lie to get what they want and then they disappear.
- There are very few good men out there now.
- The quality of men has dropped in the world.
- Every time I date a man, I'm disappointed and left having to pull together the pieces of my soul. I just don't know if I can do that anymore.
- I'm happier on my own focusing on myself.
- It takes me a long time to trust a man now.

Actually, if you're in the pattern of attracting these types of men and women in your life and this is what you believe, then it says more about you than it does about the men and women in the world. Men in their woundedness. Women in their woundedness. Projecting at one another what they fear and believe about love from the perspective of their past experiences. Attracting and pursuing this same energy over and over again in others as a result because of their view of the world. If we look below the surface of what I hear so often from men and women, what is it that we can see?

A burning desire for the same things. Love.
To feel appreciated. Freedom.
Not to cheat or be disloyal, but to just be themselves. Understanding.
Safety. Peace. Security.
Room for growth.

I invite you to lose your judgement and criticism of the opposite sex and to instead see the similarities. To stop needing the opposite sex to be different or better for you and to see the potential for good and amazing in them. They just are what they are. A soul desiring to be loved, to connect and to be valued like you. Just moving in a different way than you do. Neither better nor more evolved than the other. Both evolving in their own way. There are going to be some of the opposite sex who are going to be good for you. And there are going to be some who are not. There will be some who will bring out the best in you and some who will not. This says nothing about the entire opposite sex. It speaks only to the individual. See the similarities.

49
WHAT WE NEED TO UNDERSTAND ABOUT OURSELVES AS HUMANS

When the soul knows something is off in a relationship, nothing you do can make that feeling go away. It will disturb your gut, it will set up shop in your mind, it will put a tonne of weight on your heart. Until you stop ignoring it. Stop ignoring it.

What are we as humans? When I ask this question, the response is almost always centred around our physical body and our physical representation as a human. And yes, we are that. Our physical human body is that of a Homosapien. We all have a body and a brain with a thinking capacity and the ability for speech that makes us entirely unique. However, to look at a human with only its physical body as its representation is to dismiss the real essence of what makes us fully human. It is to dismiss the magic. The soul.

Quantum physics can now tell us when the soul and our consciousness, enters the human body at the moment of conception. We see it in the petri dish during the IVF process. At the beautiful moment of conception there is a halo that can now be seen in the lab when the sperm enters the egg. At that moment, scientists know that the cell is viable, meaning it will grow into a foetus. The halo is indicative of the strength of the cell (the cell now called a zygote, the beginnings of cells becoming a human), and they use this indicator to choose the strongest one in the petri dish to transfer into the mother during the IVF process.

That halo moment has been identified as the moment the soul enters the zygote. It is the moment that the wonderful uniqueness that is you enters the beginnings of the growth of your physical body. This is the point where science in many ways meets religion and spirituality, whatever your beliefs might be. Your soul energy enters your physical body at conception. You are made up of two separate parts. You are the soul. And you are the physical body. Science can show us now that we are more than just our physical bodies. We are energy that is taken from the energy present around us at the point of our conception, which is then placed into a body of mass, the beginnings of our physical body. A quantum biologist whose work I love, Dr Courtney Hunt, explains this beautifully, almost like our souls having made its way to the front of the queue at a deli counter. We're given a number, your number is eventually called, you approach the counter and into the world you enter to become Susan Smith, whose physical human body will look like this, whose parents are Bob and Jane.

The magic of human existence. To ask ourselves how destined were we to become what we one day grow up to become? How much of our soul journey was already mapped out for us before we entered our human physical form? Why is any of this relevant to this book? Because today we see so many humans mostly leading their lives from the point of their human physical body, achieving, thriving, doing what is right, responsible, financially smart. While all along mostly or completely ignoring their soul, how they feel, their intuition, their emotional world, what they actually desire and are drawn to. Until it becomes a scream. We see a big disconnect in many humans now where much of their life and decision making is made from a point of their brain and humanness. And very little, sometimes none, is made from the point of their soul.

Divorce for many adults is the pivot point where the soul became so unhappy and felt so out of alignment with the physical human world and relationships created around it that it could no longer be ignored or quietened. For some it feels like the first major pivot point in their life. However, if most of us look back with eyes now wide open, we can see other moments in our younger years, before social constructs of marriage, finance and responsibility were built up around us so heavily, where we made life decisions from our point of soul desire and for no other reason than because we desired to. The teen or twenty-year-old person who moves interstate or overseas to travel, to take a gap year or to follow love is a wonderful example here. A life decision to leave a marriage is made from a point of someone's soul. Whether someone chooses to continue to lead with their soul in life after divorce or to even awaken to their soul as a result of it … well that's another journey.

It's why some people go on to change quite deeply as a person after a marriage ends. Their values change, what is important to them evolves, they begin to look at their patterns and heal their wounds, they begin the process of waking up to themselves and the beliefs that lead them to become who they are. For these individuals, life often completely changes after a divorce. Their ideal partner changes too. It's also why some people don't change at all after a divorce. They have no desire to change. They go onto meet the same kinds of partners next with the same kinds of dynamics that allows them to stay the same kind of person. Their soul never really awakened. Maybe it did for a moment, enough for them to recognise their dissatisfaction and misalignment with their human physical world, enough to propel them forward. Only for them to return back to leading with their humanness again. Have you seen yourself or your ex-partner in this yet?

50

WHY FINDING LOVE AFTER DIVORCE IS A DIFFERENT KIND OF LOVE JOURNEY

We have an unfortunate growing culture that fosters and celebrates outward success, possessions and technology, while downplaying the needs and desires of our inner world. We can see this in both younger and older generations. But increasingly in the younger now with the oversaturation of social media in our lives. What someone is wearing, driving, where they live, what they own, how they look, where they tag themselves on social media. All glimpses into where they are holidaying and eating out without telling you where they are. A glimpse of the label that they are wearing without telling you what they're wearing. Can we collectively lol at the human race and ourselves right now?

All of these facets just add to the human physical form, which is ultimately, to me, the avatar we use to present to the world how we desire to be perceived by others. Material comforts are great to a point, of course. Yes, they are also sometimes necessary. But without a foundation of connection, love and inner satisfaction, life and its meaning can begin to feel quite lacking. Disconnected. Fake. Still, it feels not enough. We can see this demonstrated in couples who outwardly have it all, success, security, the beautiful home, family and life but who are nevertheless dissatisfied and feel a sense of disconnect and emptiness with it all.

Often, it's not until we leave a marriage that we are able to step back and take a look at what really played. What you both really prioritised. What that says about you. What it says about them. What it says about you both as a couple.

Understanding where we went off our soul path and why. Working through the internal beliefs and conditioning we hold and breaking down the human barriers present within us. All of this is us taking down the shield that life has built up around our heart and soul. This is no snapping of the fingers, no overnight process. This is an undoing process that occurs slowly over time. A gradual lowering of our protective shield, of our need to be seen and perceived in a certain way. A growing comfortableness to be seen for who we really are. A process that in time returns us home to the beautiful loving soul we are and always were before the world happened to us, back to the soul that we were when we took our first breath. Innocent, loving, carefree, trusting, adventurous, playful. This process of undoing allows us a greater capacity for self-love and love to others. This opens us to new deeper and more meaningful connection with ourselves and our next partner in the process.

This is why finding love after divorce is a different journey and process to the one that led you to find a partner to marry. Everyone was leading with their humanness and their physical body to procreate, settle, succeed and thrive when they chose a partner to marry in their twenties and thirties.

We can look at the adult modern dating world after divorce and see three types of people we will encounter in the dating process. Some leading entirely from their physical body and ego, unaware of their soul, unaware that they're living from their conditioning and fear. Awakening humans of different with varying levels and degrees, leading somewhat from their physical body and ego, and increasingly leading more from their soul. And awake humans, leading and living entirely from their soul, their physical world and relationships built around them in such a way that it supports their soul and its growth. A sliding scale of awakening humans, egos and souls bumping their hearts and bodies into one another. Sometimes for a long time, sometimes for a brief time. Some mindlessly. Chasing the next hot thing or catch. Some evolving upwards to love, learning lessons along the way through the contrast of negative and positive experiences. Some of them doing this consciously. Some of them asleep to it all. Hurting others and themselves along the way. A mixed bag. None of this journey or level of awareness was needed for us to find a partner to marry. But if we wish to create a different future than the past and the relationship we have left behind, then this is your journey now, to evolve up.

51
IS THE GRASS ACTUALLY GREENER

If ever I am having a session with a client who is weighing up whether to leave their marriage or not, this statement is almost always asked. Is the grass actually greener? Will I actually be better off? And my children too? Shouldn't I just be grateful with what I have? Will it even be worth it? The answer is quite simply that it depends on what you want. It depends on what you currently have. Do you want more of the same with your partner for the rest of your life or do you not? At some point in all of our relationships, we must accept that the people we are in a relationship with might change a little bit, but not that much. They are who they are, and you are innately who you are. And while almost everyone goes on to mature and evolve into themselves as they age, very rarely does someone change personalities and their characteristics entirely.

They are who they are, and you are innately who you are, and together you bring out certain elements and different qualities in each other. We all know through experience that there are some relationships in our life that bring out more of our better qualities without trying. These relationships feel easy, and the connection just flows. And some relationships bring out more of our negative qualities without trying. These relationships can feel like harder, heavier work. Something that many of us like to forget is that we get to choose our life experience and the relationships we keep in our lives. In fact, our relationships form one of the biggest pieces in the jigsaw puzzle of our life experience. Some of you haven't been growing in your life because your biggest roadblock was in the bed next to you every night. Or they still are! You get to choose. So yes, the grass can actually be greener. In fact, it almost always is.

I don't personally know of many, if any, divorced individuals, and I know a lot through my work, who regret their decision, wishing they could reverse their decision and go back. This is a fear question. They look to their separated and divorced friends and depending on their social circle and perception, will see what they want to see. Women will see girlfriends who are still single and wading through the dating world and think 'not worth it' because she's alone. They do this while completely overlooking the fact that this woman might feel frustrated with not having found a great man yet, yes, but who is deeply loving her life, her freedom and wouldn't change a thing. She hasn't found him yet. It's not a forever situation. She would never choose to go back. And men will see friends who lost at least half of their everything that they built up and created, out there and dating the hot new chick only for it to go pear-shaped quickly and so they think 'not worth it' also because he's now alone. They do this while completely overlooking the fact that this man might feel frustrated with not having found a woman yet, yes, but who is deeply loving his life, his freedom and wouldn't change a thing. He hasn't found her yet. It's not a forever situation. Unhappy and dissatisfied married people like to forget that it's not a forever situation for their divorced friends. It's just a moment in time. It's very hard to perceive how life could look while anyone is in something that they're tolerating and settling because of future fears of what-ifs and what could go wrongs.

Recently, I was out socially with a girlfriend, and she ran into a group of school mums that she hadn't seen since she left her husband. One mum came up to her and after some initial small talk said with a face full of empathy, 'How are you with everything? Have you been okay? You poor thing.' My girlfriend replied that she was fantastic, feeling better than ever, had met a new partner and that everything was going great. When this woman left and returned back to her table my girlfriend turned to me and said, 'That's so bizarre, she's in an unhappy marriage, they've been in separate bedrooms, living separate lives for years and she's worried about me? I'm worried about her!' It's all relative, isn't it? The pain and dissatisfaction we choose to live with, accept and accommodate as normal.

I always like to put it this way to my clients. If I projected everyone forward, whether divorced or married and imagined them all thirty to forty years on, where would they all be? I'm certain that those who are now divorced and looking for love will have found their someone to love. They will have found their way and love will have come around again for them in a newly evolved and loving way, aligned more than ever with who they had grown into being. And those who are married and who continue to stay married to the same person will with almost certainty still be experiencing their relationship with a similar tone and shade as they are living it today. We know this to be likely true because they will be the same two people with the same similar and established patterns of behaviour with the same ways of bringing the good and the not-so-good qualities out in one another as they always have. If I look to my girlfriend and her school mum friend, how might that look and transpire? Almost certainly the school mum friend will be in the same situation with her husband if not worse into the future. And my girlfriend? She will be happy and have continued moving on with her life and forming relationships and experiences that are an amazing fit for who she is now.

We get to choose our life experience. We get to choose who we keep in it. Particularly within that inner sanctum of people we hold close to us. We really do.

52

LOVE AFTER DIVORCE AND LOVE WITHIN A MARRIAGE

The beautiful energy of the love that comes after a divorce is that it's a choice. A choice to be with someone because there is nowhere else you desire to be. Someone is there because they fully desire to be with you. Not because they are tied to another and have to be. There are very few marriages where both individuals, hand on heart, could say that. Sadly, this is how marriages can so easily support toxic and negative behaviours. Cheating. Affairs. Emotional and physical abuse. Keeping someone stuck in a repeated cycle of it all.

Even for the person who has fallen out of love with their partner, where the above dynamics aren't present, the ties that bind within a marriage can still feel suffocating. They feel trapped to remain in the union even though their heart is no longer fully in it. For the individual in a marriage like this, it can feel hard to leave. Someone in a marriage can sadly have the potential to get away with so much if they exhibit this personality, particularly if they know the other individual will more than likely never leave them because they love the family unit, the lifestyle that has been established, the dream they still believe in or because they know their self-worth and confidence is low. Marriage for an abuser or a selfish person is the perfect playing ground to get away with it all and to have their cake of safety and security too.

The dating world after divorce is often talked about with much negativity. Men treating women badly and vice versa. I can't deny that, in many ways, there is a shade of this: neither sex understanding nor fully appreciating the other. But are many marriages around you, and the behaviours persisting in them, all that much better in behaviour than what we see in single and dating people? Really? Those who behave badly are deservedly dumped or they move on to a next relationship to play out again their old patterns and conditioning is the only difference in the dating pool. Instead of taking out their lack of growth and self-awareness on one person, they're taking it out on many, leaving a trail of hurt and broken hearts. The only pathway to rise above this car crash? To not participate in it. To come to a relationship as a more self-aware, conscious version of yourself over being an asleep less aware version of yourself. To date, be in love and be in a relationship from a place of soul not from your humanness.

53
LIFE PATHS AND SOUL JOURNEYS

This is not the book to explore where does the soul come from or even what exists beyond the soul. I need you to only accept or be open to accepting that the soul exists as a separate entity within the human body. You are your human body. And you are your soul. The human body exists as the vehicle for your soul. Two separate parts. Science is aware of this and is trying to capture and learn more about the soul's entry into the human body at a centre called the European Council for Nuclear Research (CERN) in Switzerland. CERN is the site of a large underground hadron collider. The world's largest and highest energy particle collider that lies in a tunnel 27 kilometres in circumference and is as deep as 175 metres beneath the France-Switzerland border. Inside the hadron collider protons and electrons are smashed together at the speed of light to create black holes into the universe, simulating the halo that occurs when the sperm and egg collide at conception, a process that also occurs at the speed of light. This isn't the book to discuss the implications for humanity if scientists manage to capture on their computers and understand the process behind how the soul comes to enter the physical body. Conceptually, once captured and understood, the soul can be captured and steered into any form on purpose. Not just a human body. Sci-fi coming to life. There is a reason why they call this discovery 'The God Particle'. So, let's just allow ourselves to sit with the unknown of this.

We know the soul exists. We know it comes from the energy around us at the point of conception but we're not sure where from precisely, though there are many theories. At conception, the energy around us enters the mass of who we are as a newly forming physical body.

At our death, the energy within us leaves the physical mass of our body and returns to the energy existing around us. Mass returning to energy. This is quantum physics. What I do believe is this. Every soul comes to Earth with a potential in front of them. In many ways pre-ordained and in many ways perhaps quite laid out for us. If we come from the energy around us at the point of our entry into the physical human world, then there is space for the argument that astrology and a reading of the planets at your time of birth might warrant some investigation, even for the most sceptic. And that anything related to energy healing of our soul body might also hold some weight. Despite my own belief in free will allowing me choice in life over my life being completely mapped out for me from birth as fate, perhaps despite your own, we have to also leave space for the beautiful magic of synchronicities, coincidences and divine timings. Because for even the most rational, logical minded individual we must allow space for the magic of life seemingly always being able to take us to where we needed to be. Shaping us to become who we were meant to be. And we have to do this because most of us have experienced cases of this. Those moments where everything came together for us at the right time, at the right place. Better than we could have ever orchestrated for ourselves. There is something in all of that.

Why come to Earth as a soul then? Who knows. There are many theories on this also. But what feels intuitively right for me is that souls come to Earth with a potential to reach. And that it is our free will as to how long it takes for us to arrive there, what detours we have along the way and ultimately whether we face the soul lessons and growth we need to master to reach our potential. We are either in alignment with our soul potential and in the slipstream of everything coming to us that is destined for us and that we deserve as a consequence, or we are out of alignment with it. In soul alignment, our life, relationships and careers feel easeful. It feels like we're in our zone and they leave us feeling happy and at peace from a deep place within. We are lit up doing what we love and by living our life. Out of soul alignment is where everything feels like hard work, a burden, a chore, where nothing is really coming together for us. We see this modelled in those individuals in life who sadly never meet their potential. The family member or friend who fell into drugs or alcohol and their potential and life was wasted as a result. Their addiction wasn't their soul potential or journey. That was their free will getting in the way of their potential. That was them ignoring the soul growth and lessons they needed to have to evolve forwards in life having overcome their addictions.

Am I explaining myself well to you? I know you came here for love and to understand more about the process of finding love after divorce. Why it feels harder. Why some loves and relationships have affected you like they have. And here I am explaining to you the soul. Why am I talking to you about this? Because if you have been through a divorce and left a marriage it is because the relationship was no longer in alignment with your soul. Or if someone left you it was because you were no longer in alignment with their soul. It is a soul journey and it's important we understand that. Because everything that needed to be learnt or could be learnt in the relationship with one another was learnt, and someone evolved out as a result.

Finding the one after divorce for you is going to need you to be living your life while being in the slipstream of your soul path, and in alignment with who you really are which can only ever take you to your fullest potential. That is the path where you will find the one, yes. It's also the path of least resistance where everything will come to you in flow that will lead you to your greatest potential and the freedom of your soul expression. You are destined to be who you are meant to be, meeting the soul who loves and celebrates you. Love lit up. Power couples that light the way for others as much as themselves. Living their soul life paths.

After leaving a marriage, the journey for many is going to first require you to find and be in the slipstream of your soul path and to be in alignment with who you really are first, sometimes for the very first time as an adult now that everything that was not that has been released. If you've left a marriage or found yourself contemplating leaving a marriage for many years without having left yet, then you will know that the thought and process of leaving feels daunting, overwhelming, stressful and brings up all of your self-doubts and fears. This is why. You are realigning back onto your soul-path. You are changing lanes on the one you were previously on. Or if someone left you. They are forcing you to.

54
THERE ARE ATTRACTIVE PEOPLE EVERYWHERE BUT SOUL CONNECTIONS ARE RARE

I walk through life and am regularly drawn to attractive people. Women who are stunning. The way they dress or look. The way they hold themselves. They catch my eye, and I appreciate them. Compare myself even. Men who are handsome and attractive. The tone of their voice. Their build. How they are living their life. They catch my eye, and I appreciate them. I appreciate their human physical form and how they present themselves. But this doesn't always translate to me being drawn to them as a person as a soul. When we recognise this as we become more self-aware and accepting during the finding love after divorce journey, we must accept this.

There is a large quantity of people out there. But the quality of soul that is going to resonate with your soul… that is much rarer. I'd love for you to be less bothered by this lack of quantity for you and to embrace more the rare magic of quality, deep soul connections. Their rarity speaks to their precious nature. Soul connections that become love connections are rare. And this is actually perfect. They would not be magic if they weren't.

55

ONE LAST THING IN CASE YOU FEEL GUILT ABOUT DIVORCE AND ITS EFFECT ON YOUR CHILDREN

You can either model to your children true love or you can model to them you're conditioning for them to replicate. Before I continue, I want to share that I am very much pro-family and a mum to two daughters. I am also a child of divorced parents. I deeply value the family unit. My support of divorce and belief that for some individuals leaving a marriage is the best, most freeing thing they could do for themselves is not because I am not pro-family. What we must see and realise is that love and family can continue to exist without marriage. In some instances, once the love and the family has evolved, the children and adults can be and are better for it. Through my many years of coaching clients through separations and my own, there a several consistent themes. If there was a dynamic of lack of love, lying, cheating, manipulation, avoidance, downplaying of your intuition and feelings to keep the peace, distrust, control or emotional abuse in your marriage, then your children were picking up on this emotional tone, this dynamic and the communication patterns and behaviours that go along with it, without you realising that they were. Often without them even realising, they were being affected and shaped by it, regardless of how good a job you felt you were doing at hiding it from them.

What are we really teaching our children when we stay in a marriage for them? We are teaching and showing them how to repress their emotions to keep the peace. We are modelling to them what love is not. We are teaching and showing them that their needs are not important in a relationship. We are shielding them from the emotional reality of life, that not all marriages and connections last forever and that is okay. It's not a failure or a poor reflection on you. We are showing our children what it looks like to self-abandon by living vicariously through them and for them instead of equally for ourselves and our partner. We are teaching them to fear, and resist change over modelling to them how to handle change with growth, grace and resilience. In some families we are modelling to them that lifestyle, possessions, keeping money together and the social façade intact is more important than the real elements that should be present in a relationship.

We are, in essence, conditioning our children to buy into and believe in the social construct of marriage that has made us feel trapped, stuck, unappreciated. We are teaching them to choose relationships and stay married for all the wrong reasons. I hear from many men and women the deep guilt and sadness they feel for their family unit breaking up and changing as well as their worries about the negative impact that this will have on their children's lives. But I would like you to begin considering the opposite: the negative impact staying in your marriage would have had on them into the future. I very much understand your feelings and fears around this. My own guilt and sadness, with a healthy dose of fear around what leaving my marriage would do to my children, was one of the main factors that made me hesitant to leave. As a product of divorced parents, it was also a desire and dream that I'd held to be able to provide my children with that ideal home and family unit that I didn't have. We actually had a relatively happy family life in the years of my marriage. My children were young when we separated and to them, we always presented as happy, loving parents. But it was all for them. And that wasn't healthy for them or anyone. As responsible adults, we must honestly sit with ourselves and ask what we are modelling and teaching our children and consider if we would want to see our future grown-up children in a marriage like ours.

When many couples do separate, often the children are either not that surprised or they have to adjust to seeing their mum and dad in future relationships with a new partner and behaving like someone in love does, intimate, touching one another, private moments just about them, being close. This is often a side they haven't seen completely in their mum or dad before. It is untrue to say that children from homes where parents are still married and together are better for it or more well-adjusted. This is a rubbish, outdated narrative. It is not always true. Many children are much better off emotionally in the long-term as a result of their parents separating. Yes, in those instances where parents were unhappily married and warring, but also in those marriages that were disconnected, loveless and too heavily focused on the children and their happiness. We start to really live the example that we want for our children after a divorce and what we know to be true for ourselves. We stop trying to facilitate their soul life path to the abandonment of our own. And, most importantly, we are being authentic. Something I can say hand on heart is that my daughters are better off now for witnessing the woman that I am today, a woman I could never have been in my marriage, in character, behaviour or mindset.

One of the most important character attributes we can model to our children is to live true to ourselves and as the best version of ourselves. And to love and be loved by another in the same way that we would love them to be.

56
WHAT DOES A NEXT-LEVEL RELATIONSHIP LOOK LIKE

For many divorced people the path to finding love again starts with them first waking up to what love and a quality relationship really is. All we know is what we have known. A sad truth for some of us to admit if all we have known is disappointment and a feeling of being let down, constrained or abandoned by love. I hear all the time, relationships are hard work, they're not meant to be easy, relationships take a lot of compromise. But are they really? Because if someone says this to me then I automatically know that theirs is that to them. But does that mean that all relationships are characterised like this for others or should be? Ah no. I don't think so. This is simply a reflection of their personal experience of relationships.

The journey to finding love after divorce almost always starts with a complete waking up to the dynamics of our past relationships and to what love and a quality next-level relationship actually is. A next-level relationship is not perfect. It is, however, easy by its nature. Not because one or both are keeping the peace to make it so. Not because someone is over-compromising on their needs. Instead, it is complementary. It is easeful. It is characterised by evolving as a soul and shedding our negative patterns and behaviours, not circling around them again. And it celebrates both individuals for all of who they are, the light and the dark.

What are the qualities of a next-level relationship?
- The relationship is the easiest part of your life. Work can feel heavy, kids can be hard, but the relationship is the easeful energy in your life.

- Safe to express anything. No need to censor yourself or downplay what you need to express.
- Sex gets hotter. Deeper. More intimate. More exploratory even.
- Couples rarely, if ever, argue.
- No compromises. Certainly not on values and matters that are important to you because you are aligned.
- Communication gets better. When you are safe to express anything, you are free to communicate without hesitation. Therefore, it only continues to open up.
- Safe to grow and there are no limits placed on who you need to be for the love and relationship to continue.
- The relationship always feels safe. You know your person is never going anywhere. There is no fear of their energy or presence leaking out to another. They don't desire to be anywhere else.

Often when we read through a list such as this it can lead us to question if such a relationship like this even exist? I want to answer that yes, it does. But this quality of a relationship is not possible with every soul that we meet. Not every soul will be a complement like this for us. This soul will be unique. And the wonderful essence about this discovery process is the soul that isn't for you will be the soul complement for someone else. No soul is left unloved. If only we kept venturing forward with an open heart, willing to keep doing so, awake and leading from the point of their soul. Letting go of people in our life if we needed to until the right soul eventually found their place with you.

57
WHAT DO WE DESIRE FROM LOVE

There are the physical and character attributes that are important, unique deal breakers to you. The one attribute we often forget is someone who will grow with me. And if someone doesn't say this to me, I actually suggest it to them by asking, because this attribute is that important. Is someone who will grow with you important? The answer is always yes. This almost always comes from a place of having outgrown someone in the past. They didn't do the work or perhaps tried to but weren't able to maintain it long-term. Slipping back into their previous patterns that exist within their comfort zone after a time.

In the first five years post my divorce, I grew out of every long-term relationship that I had. We would start on the same page when we met, only to end up later, still in the same book, only now chapters behind to where I was. If we acknowledge how hard it is to grow and change as individuals, then we have to accept how absolutely impossible, sometimes futile, a process it is to try and motivate or even carry someone over the line to grow and change. Trying to help somebody who isn't ready or open is literally like trying to push porridge up a hill. Exhausting. Hard. Constant work. Someone has to want to do it for themselves. This pattern of growing out of different relationships in our lives is indicative of the soul's growth through love. It's where the love journey can start to feel hard or disappointing for some. And it's where I would love to introduce to you the three types of love that spiritually exist for all of us on our journeys.

1. **Soulmates**
2. **Karmic Loves**
3. **Twin Flames (or 'the one')**

You will out-grow a soulmate. You will also out-grow a karmic love. But you will not out-grow a twin flame connection. In this connection you will inspire positive growth in one another.

This is the conscious desire of love: to be in union with one another and to continue to have the freedom to grow, love, express and evolve alongside one another while continuing to inspire and bring out the positive in one another. Beautiful.

58

SOULMATE LOVE: THE PERSON FAMILY AND SOCIETY CONDITIONED US TO BRING HOME

You will meet many soulmates in your life, and they will come in many different forms. Souls you feel deeply connected with that are comfortable, safe, where you feel at home. Your soulmate is actually not your one. This angers a lot of married people when I say this. It triggers all their fears around security, safety and certainty that they have placed around their marriage. It also knocks them off their pedestal of somehow being in a better life position than a divorced person. But their anger or opinions don't make it any less true.

Your soulmate is not your one, as comfortable as they might feel to you. In an intimate relationship, this is often the first major long-term relationship we experience. This is the fairytale of boy meets girl, marries and lives happily-ever-after that we read about as children. Before we really know ourselves, but while we are at an age to reproduce, we unwittingly follow the expectations of what our families hope and expect for us, who society and our social circle expect us to end up with, our genetic and socio-economic equal. Even our own personal belief that it's time to settle will influence this choice in a relationship.

It is love. It is a deep connection. But it is a love that we often outgrow because of the foundations listed above and the reasons why this love came together in the first place. Whether we choose to leave, or stay is very much the personal soul journey and choice of both individuals in this relationship. One might recognise that they've outgrown the relationship while the other is happily comfortable in it.

From the outside looking in, regardless of how an individual might feel in it, this relationship simply looks right. It is the relationship that family and our social circle expected us to be in or hoped for us to have. It feels safe. It brings comfort. It feels familiar. And it is usually supported by our social and family connections around us which keeps everything feeling bound together. This can be a nice feeling for someone comfortably married into this. A suffocating one for someone who no longer wants to be married into it. The best analogy I've heard used to describe this dynamic came from a male friend of mine who is in a soulmate relationship, cheats on his wife regularly but doesn't leave for reasons of friendship, love for his wife and for reasons of finances:

My marriage feels like a warm bath. It's not so hot that I have to get out and it's not so cold that it's uncomfortable to stay in. I'm not completely happy. But I'm not unhappy either. I could be happier and more in love. I could be unhappier.

Being with our soulmate makes us feel like we're following the rules of success that we've been given for love and life. It feels safe. With soulmate love, both individuals stay the same and don't evolve out of their conditioning too much which is the requirement for this connection to continue in comfort. However, it is as we evolve, through age and life experience, when we start to see soulmates outgrowing one another. In this space, the one evolving and outgrowing either curtails their soul growth so as not to outgrow the connection for reasons of love, safety, security, family or finances. Or they leave the connection. This is where we see individuals trying to keep a lid on their inner world and their feelings of discontent and disconnection to maintain the relationship. This is where someone can accidentally (or purposefully) fall into an affair, or many affairs, either emotional or physical. Their inner world is in turmoil and conflict, whether they have conscious soul awareness of it or not.

Someone here might say it was just physical, or it didn't mean anything, but I would like to counter with you that neither statement is completely true. Both statements are simply a reflection of their own lack of inner awareness and lack of soul awakening in themselves. There was a soul desire or need behind it, whatever that might have been. To end our soulmate relationship is often to go against the expectations and hopes for us and to break free from what we were supposed to do, often disappointing those we love most in the process. Leaving a soulmate relationship that is bound by marriage and getting a divorce in the process merely exaggerates all of this. The ties that bind emotionally, socially and in a familial sense run deep. Soulmate love is safe and feels familiar and it's why some of us have difficulty moving on from this love even when we feel elements of disconnect in the connection.

You can see now why many prefer the comfort of staying. Better what they know than the unknown of what they don't and to potentially disappoint others in the process. Early on in these relationships we see glimpses of why things won't ultimately work out. But often we are so in our head, at the time to be able to fully see past ourselves. And as the relationship progresses, we find ourselves having walked too far down the path of living the dream we once laid out for ourselves to want to now see it or feel we can go back. These individuals close themselves to the pull of the soul journey. Soulmate relationships are based on comfort. There is not the sharing of the mesmerising energy ties present in twin flame relationships.

Individuals who choose to leave a soulmate relationship do so because they come to realise the relationship is holding them back from experiencing the next level of life and love. The price of staying in the relationship begins to feel too heavy for them to continue. If you have left a relationship or marriage to a soulmate, whether by choice or consequence, someone followed their soul voice to do so. It started a soul journey. How you choose to walk it is your path, from your point of humanness or from your soul. The choice is yours.

59

KARMIC LOVE: THE LOVES THAT TEACH US THE LESSONS WE DON'T WANT TO HAVE

This is the love we are seeing mostly played out in the modern dating world. Karmic love is the cause of the car crash present in today's dating sphere. A soul beginning a new relationship before healing wounds from the past. All souls of varying levels of awareness and awakening, growing and evolving through love. All of them, learning on one another as part of their soul evolution. This is what we call a karmic cycle and it's one that many divorced people find themselves in. We can experience multiple karmic partners in our lifetime. Not because our one is not out there, but because we're not ready for our one. Perhaps there are other growth pathways that need to be explored, more lessons to master. Elements that when brought together in time will make you a whole, shining version of yourself first. Karmic love is a process of ascension.

It is common for us to have as many karmic loves as it takes until we see and heal the voids within our soul. The voids that many of us attempted to fill through our soulmate relationship. A need to not be alone or rejected. A need to people-please. A fear of security and not being able to provide for ourselves financially. Low self-worth. Lack of confidence. A want to be rescued. A lack of inner balance and purpose. Using sex as a way to avoid emotional depth and intimacy. This is why dating after divorce can look like a car crash, they are oblivious to the soul journey that is actually shaping their love choices and behaviour.

Karmic loves teach us not to look for someone to make us feel better about ourselves or to give us a sense of belonging or self-worth.

Karmic loves teaches us to be strong, shows us old patterns so that we can change who we attract, which means we first need to change the energy of who we are and how we move through love and the world. And it will keep doing this, over and over again, in as many different partners as necessary, until we wake up to the lessons and growth we need to have. Karmic loves are painful like that. This love shines a light on the gaps within our soul and because we are in the process of awakening and evolving, this is why we so often project and see these loves as our forevers. Our one.

These relationships are so close to our ideal, minus a few red flags that we've downplayed often from the beginning because everything else was so damn right. This is the relationship that comes in when we feel we've done enough work, when we feel we've had enough time on our own, when we think we're ready. Only to realise … no, this isn't quite true.

The end of a karmic love relationship is one of the most painful on the journey to finding the one because we realise, we haven't come as far as we've hoped. The ending can literally bring you to your knees. They mirror back to us how wounded we still are and how much growing we still have to do, not just in terms of our intimate relationships, but also in our personal development. This relationship teaches us that there is no short cut, as much as we might try. The effect of the karmic love process cycling through the adult, post-divorce dating pond is significant. It's why many start to feel a sense of hopelessness when it comes to love. The hurt from these relationships can feel so soul destroying that people give up on love, decide they'd rather stay single, or even choose to only pursue the physical. Yet, we must realise the desire to settle down after divorce is different now than it was prior to getting married. Everyone has already left a love that led them to have to compromise, put their needs to the side or that has cost them emotionally, financially and socially.

Now, someone is going to have to really capture their attention, awaken something within, stir their soul in such a way that it makes them want to stop swiping, stop looking around and to feel that they have met such a person that is so unique they couldn't possibly let it go. Spiritually, we call this person our twin flame. The one. Karmic love is an addictive love. Twin flame love is a whole other level. It is magnetic because of the energy they have and bring out in one another.

Whether someone is awake to the process or not, love after divorce is a soul journey that some will experience consciously or not. Now you can experience it consciously and not lose hope because you can see it for the process that it is. Each love is teaching us something. Sometimes painfully, because we so desperately wanted it to work and for them to be the one. Each love is ascending us higher in ourselves and on our path. But there is light. The more open and awake we stay to this process of soul growth and alignment, the faster we will ascend through it towards the love that will rock our world, wake us even further and that will grow with us, over us outgrowing it.

Twin flame love.
Your energetic match.
Cut from the same soul and split in two.

The ultimate power couple in love and life that inspires others around them with their love, sometimes even with their message and the way they choose to live. These couples exist as the reminder of what is real, true and possible in a loving relationship. Of what we deserve and desire. Not everyone believes in the concept of twin flames, but I believe it to be true.

I counter that we don't see as many of these power couples in life as we should because not everyone continues to walk this path with an open heart. Many settle and compromise before they find their twin flame. They give up on this love before they arrive. Or they stay in a discontented marriage and choose to not follow the path. When you leave a marriage, you are choosing this path. You have stepped beyond your fear and conditioning. Whether you have realised it or not, you are on the soul path.

60

THE ONE BEFORE THE ONE:
THE LOVE THAT WE WANT TO WORK,
THAT SHATTERS OUR SOUL WHEN IT DOESN'T

I'm going to slide this one in here, the one before the one. This love is often the precursor to us having a dark night of the soul. A heartbreak that cuts so that deep that it leaves us questioning everything that we thought we knew about love and about ourselves. When it ends, this love can be soul shattering. The one before the one is known as the false twin flame phenomenon. The love and attraction is so deep it feels destined, and we so wish it would be, so we overlook all the reasons that show us it is not so. A false twin flame is someone that you believe is your one, but they are not. You will look back on this love and wonder how you ever believed them to be the one and why you placed them on a pedestal. Hindsight is always humbling with this one.

If drama, arguments, pain, ghosting or cheating occurs in this relationship, or if you have been the third person in their life for a period of time, without resolve or any real positive ascension or progress, then you are not with your twin flame. You are not. The entire purpose of the twin flame relationship is soul evolution in both individuals within the connection. You both inspire one another to grow and develop into the best version of yourselves. If this doesn't happen, then no matter how much you wish, hope or believe it to be so, regardless of how magnetic the sex or attraction you have with this person, you aren't with your twin flame. It is karmic love. And there are lessons here for you to learn. Twin flame love connections are rarely straightforward as you will come to understand in the next chapter. Their entrance into our life always brings with it a shaking to our core and foundations which is why this relationship can be so often associated with less-than-ideal patterns: push/pull dynamics, time together and time in separation while we process the entrance of this kind of love into our life, questioning what we want and what we're ready for and what we're going to do about this love.

A twin flame connection walks into your life and nothing is ever the same again. Even if you're not in a relationship with them. Such is the effect they will have on you until you come into union with them. My belief is that we should never give the twin flame label to anyone in our life until they are fully showing up as one. Up until that point, we should keep evolving forward in our life and only give them the label of maybe or potentially when the time reveals itself. Like it always does. We should never keep ourselves available for a connection if it is not treating us like we deserve, if it is costing us our self-worth, respect or confidence simply because we believe them to be our twin flame. That is us romanticising someone and seeing them for their potential, not their reality. This is dangerous territory. That can be us co-creating and choosing toxicity. The ending of this relationship leaves many devastated and so that they choose to stay single for a time. Eventually, after healing, we come to the full realisation that maybe there's more to life than being in a relationship anyway. And in our core, we are deeply comfortable with it.

We begin to deeply explore all the things that we love and are passionate about. The things that bring us soul joy and bring out the best in us. Us finding and being in our soul alignment. This love breaks us in such a way that it becomes the catalyst for our twin flame. Without it, we would never have desired, by our own choice, to deeply examine the parts of ourselves that need healing and opening. This love breaks us. But it also makes us.

61

TWIN FLAME LOVE: THE LOVE THAT MAKES US STOP

When we begin the journey of moving on from a marriage, we leave with a sense of hope, that love will come into our world and will be better than the one we left behind. Very rarely does anyone leave hoping for a similar shade of the same kind of relationship in the future. Certainly, no one leaves hoping for worse. We all leave hoping that in choosing ourselves we are, in essence, also choosing for ourselves and our children a better life that brings us more peace, love, soul freedom, joy and a level of abundance. Spiritually, a twin flame union is the peak union. Its entrance into our world will leave us questioning if we've ever loved before. It makes us see all of our previous love choices for what they were, our conditioning or a choice made from a place of fear.

Twin flames are the same in their soul. They are the one soul split in half. By consequence they have very similar goals, ideas, values, personalities, wants, needs and desires. This is because twin flames are naturally of a higher level of vibration, they have done or are doing the soul work to be at their best. They are of the same frequency and energy level. This is why this love has a magical spark over an addictive pull that we don't feel in other love connections. When twin flames first come together, any negative belief about love or self that they carry such as hurt, fear, emotional baggage, shame or negative patterned behaviour all comes to the surface for you to be able to relinquish. It does so because this is a different energy of love than we've ever experienced before. Everything that is not love as a result of the past can't exist here in this union. All of it comes to the surface to be cleared, and within a twin flame relationship it is cleared, remembering that by definition:

A twin flame connection is the catalyst for positive change and soul evolution in both individuals.

As one soul awakens and heals, so does the other. The entry of a twin flame connection in our life always brings with it a level of complication. This is because the entrance is typically much later on in life. Even if we may have met this person earlier in our life, it is unlikely that we will find ourselves in a relationship with our twin flame until later in life. This is because most of us wouldn't have been ready for them earlier. In order to receive our twin flame, we need to have not only cleared a large amount of our karma through previous relationships, but we need to have reached a point of more awareness and evolvement of who we are.

And so, as a result ... both individuals have almost always had children already. One or both souls may still be in another relationship or even a marriage. One or both may still be in the energy of their conditioning, of living a life of responsibility and I shoulds. Some twin flames find themselves awakening to their dissatisfaction with it all but having made none of the practical steps to change or end it. Some twin flame connections are the same sex, from different cultural or socio-economic backgrounds, living in other parts of the world, or have significant age disparities. Your twin flame is, as you can probably tell, often someone you never thought would be your type, who you could have never imagined being your person, who you never expected to feel for in the way that you do. Often our twin flame is far from our conditioned type. Even the timing of this love's entrance into your life will not make sense, though it will later. An individual's version of what love actually is will begin to be questioned when the presence of their twin flame enters their life. Their values will change and so will their view on what they want from life. Friendships and relationships will change as they begin to evolve. Some will end. Some will experience career change. Or even move cities and countries.

A twin flame's presence truly awakens your soul. It is a process of awakening to love and self and once started, will not be stopped. And so, their entrance into your life becomes a marker of time—before them, and life after them—because you and your life are never the same ever again. From the beginning when twin flames meet, even before they are in a relationship together, they will feel a deep knowing of each other, a comfort level and ease that they haven't felt with another, a freedom and acceptance to fully be themselves and a desire to just be in each other's energy. True twin flames will always return to one another, there isn't another choice. It is not an addiction. It is a pure desire to be in some way close to their counterpart and in their energy. You can't choose your twin flame or who you want it to be. Your twin flame just is who it is. You are joined on a spiritual level.

As one soul heals and awakens, so does the other. The work you do for yourself will always translate to your twin flame's growth too. You are polishing the diamond that is both of your souls. Twin flames have divine timing even if it doesn't make sense. In this connection we receive a glimpse of something that remains on our heart, a connection becomes ignited that always remains. Your feelings for a twin flame will challenge your rational brain because nothing is normal or traditional. As one of my clients so eloquently put it, 'If I leave my wife for her, it will cost me millions but if I don't do this to be with her, I'll regret it for the rest of my life.' Rather than healing our past, the growth within a twin flame union is about being able to open up to our future. It's less about who we are or were and more about the person we're meant to become.

Twin flames move through various phases that form part of the overall journey. Because they come in so unexpectedly, it often means we have to rearrange our lives. In this process of rearranging a life, yours and theirs, know a twin flame will never force you to accept less than you deserve or treat you with narcissism. But you both will challenge one another during this connection. This love is defined by stages of progression and seeming regression. Of awakening to the connection and this constant feeling of being drawn to them. Of deep passion and attraction like you've had with no other. Of feeling deeply triggered by what the other mirrors back to us. Stages of pulling away, running and chasing as the depth of the connection causes one or both to pull away, not ready to see or make the changes in their life or selves that is necessary for this relationship. Of surrendering to the union and accepting that this connection is forever instead of trying to fight it, neither has to be afraid of rejection here. All of this transpires before a union and a definitive relationship can occur.

Twin flame love and the way this connection comes together is going to be vastly different than the pathway that led you to be married. Throw every rule book out that you had about love and how it might happen for you and how it might look. Those rules don't apply here.

62

TWIN FLAME LOVE: REAL OR BULLSHIT

Twin flame love is a connection that defies logic and expectations. Until we have experienced this love it is easy to dismiss it as spiritual mumbo jumbo. You might be surprised to read this, but it actually doesn't matter what you believe here. Those who have experienced a twin flame connection, or even a false twin flame, already believe in its existence. And if you don't, that's okay.

Science will tell you that there is no scientific evidence to support this spiritual ideology. I would counter how can science talk about and dismiss the soul journey while it's still trying to understand and capture its entry into our physical human body. We don't know what we don't know. And we don't know a lot. For some who have always applied the rational, logical and the conditioned mind to love, this concept of twin flames, maybe even this concept of the soul as I've described in this book, is going to seem far-fetched. But your belief or your non-belief here doesn't actually change whether this love exists or doesn't exist. My only wish is for you to stay awake and conscious to the soul process I've shared here. For you to take your human conditioned blinkers off, to continue living your life and to choose to neither be closed or open to this twin flame concept. Rather, let's just see what happens for you now that you are aware of the concepts around soulmates, the karmic love cycle and twin flames.

Let's see what you notice now around you. How your perception of others and their behaviour begins to change. Sometimes just knowing and having the awareness changes and opens up everything.

63
ARE TWIN FLAMES TOXIC

A twin flame connection will challenge you, trigger you and mirror back to you everything you need to ascend and rise above. It becomes toxic only when one or both in the connection don't rise above. Which means it's not a twin flame connection … it's karmic. A twin flame connection is only toxic if you believe and are holding onto someone being your twin flame before they have earnt the label. And accepting and tolerating toxic behaviour in the name of someone being your twin flame is a consequence of this. This behaviour is why the twin flame connection can sometimes be given a bad name. A twin flame love and connection is meant to help you grow and evolve. Yes, it will also shine light on your shadows, wounds and conditioned beliefs that don't serve your highest soul growth.

All of this will trigger you. But no relationship should ever mistreat you. Any relationship that does is the invitation for us to step away. Even if you believe someone to be your twin flame this statement still rings true. Remember this connection is a catalyst for you to both ascend and evolve as souls. Not just one of you. If you continue to follow this path, regardless of whether you believe someone to be a twin flame connection or not, then you are always going to be safeguarding yourself by ascending yourself out of toxic behaviour.

So, allow yourself to grow and evolve over holding yourself back. And if they are truly your twin flame, then this will be the catalyst for them to also ascend. Your growth will ultimately be their growth too.

64

HOW TO KNOW IF SOMEONE IS YOUR TWIN FLAME

The twin flame relationship doesn't have to be difficult. Twin flame relationships are an entirely different energy and union. When together, they make love look easy, which often leads one or the other to initially believe that it won't last or possibly continue like this. Twin flame connections are certainly not one defined by compromise, settling or keeping the peace in the way so many marriages are defined. The only difficulty we bring and create around our twin flame connection is our desire for it to be in our lives when it isn't or for it to be further along than where it is. We must see a twin flame for what it is: a love that doesn't follow the same pathway as the previous loves we've known and is ultimately a reflection of the soul work that both still need to do.

Common indicators of the twin flame relationship:
- A knowingness and interest in one another from the first moment of meeting.
- A bond and connection that is unexplainable and unlike anything else you have experienced.
- You are finely tuned to each other's energies and emotions. Intuitively you just know.
- Their presence in your life is a catalyst for you to both grow and evolve positively towards your fullest potential.
- You are a mirror for each other's fears and desires.
- Explosive chemistry and a strong physical attraction.
- Overwhelming feeling of unconditional love. You know they will never judge you or reject you.

- The entrance of their love into your life wakes you up and creates a complete upheaval in your life.
- In the early stages of the relationship, you become scared of the relationship and want to bail.
- You never have to put on a show for them. You can be your authentic self.
- A feeling you have known one another in previous lifetimes.
- Shared values, beliefs, lifestyles and points of view.
- Unconditional love and an understanding of one another.
- You feel a sense of completion and peace in having found each other.
- A desire to be close to one another and to remain in each other's lives.
- Intimacy and friendship on all levels is unparalleled.
- Meeting this person perpetuates a spiritual awakening in both of you.
- Neither of you are ever the same person again for all the right reasons.

As you can see, twin flame love. It is no ordinary love. It is entirely unique. Its existence is disbelieved and doubted by those who haven't discovered it along their life path as yet but believed and accepted by those who have. These are the people who have experienced the magnetic pull and lived the catalytic effect that came with the entrance of their twin flame into their life. Something they never asked for that changed their perspective on life and love.

65

THE STAGES PRESENT WITHIN A TWIN FLAME CONNECTION

There are no guarantees or timelines when it comes to a twin flame connection. What is always true is that the entry of your twin flame into your life becomes a point of reference in your soul journey. There is the time before your twin flame entered your life. And then there is the time thereafter because nothing in your life is ever the same again. Their entry becomes a significant reference point in your life. The beginning of a true waking up to love, life and your soul's potential. And the unstoppable pull of your soul and the life force around you to lead you there. Sometimes you will feel as if it is ordained and even against your will. There is no going back to who you once were. Try as you might. This is the distinction of a twin flame connection, it is a catalyst for positive growth for both individuals. This is inevitable because both have awakened to the elements within themselves and the aspects of life that are not in alignment with them. Neither can go back to living how they did before.

While the twin flame relationship can be intense and difficult at first, they still treat you with love. Love is always present. Love always remains throughout the stages of this connection that I will share with you below. Be aware of your ego attaching itself to someone who you think is your twin flame when in fact love is not present, does not remain and there is not positive growth.

TWIN FLAME RELATIONSHIP STAGES:

1. Signs and synchronicities that a big change is coming into your life.

2. The recognition of your twin flame. A desire to be in one another's energy. To be in conversation with one another. A falling for someone harder than you expected or in a way that doesn't make rational sense.

3. Insecurities and triggering of one another. Of old wounds and beliefs. The release of what needs to be cleared in their lives so that life is in alignment for each individual within the connection. The runner and chaser dynamic can happen during this stage as an individual experiences being triggered by life or the other and as they heal from the changes arising as a result of the connection in their life.

4. Surrendering to the connection. Both stop fighting the connection and the presence of one another in their life, despite the triggering and changes that the connection brings to their life. The full acceptance of this being a unique connection in their life that neither want to relinquish.

5. Healing and growing together. A union. The allowing and settling into an unconditional love for one another. There is no dependence.

6. Oneness. Finding a shared purpose and cause for the two souls that inspires others around them. The power couple.

66
THE CREATION OF POWER COUPLES

What is my desire with this book? What do I wish to awaken within you and to inspire in humanity? The answer. My desire is to create a world that is full of more power couples living at their fullest potential instead of seeing a world full of more mediocre couples. Couples settling for and managing behaviours and circumstances that are not healthy or fulfilling for them. One of the painful aspects of my profession as a divorce coach is the social conversations that occur when a group of people who I've just met find out what my profession is. If they're divorced, their response is, 'Oh, I wish I had known about you while I was going through my own divorce.' If they're married, the response turns almost straight to their own less-than-ideal marriage dynamics and the things they have to tolerate from their husbands or wives. All interjected with self-deprecating humour, of course. Sometimes I get so tired of having to have these social conversations that I tell a little white lie when asked what I do for work, and I tell them I am a dental hygienist (my former profession). I joke that, socially, I'd rather hear about people's bad teeth than their marriage problems when I'm enjoying downtime. Both professions illicit a sharing of a story in some way. And while I smile at the wife complaining about her husband who is drinking too much again or this and that, I am looking at her and wondering something much different. I imagine where she would be in life and in herself if she wasn't trying to manage and deal with behaviour that she doesn't like and that isn't aligned with her? If she was with someone who didn't do that and behaved instead in a way that her soul desires.

Imagine what potential this woman could reach if she wasn't stuck in her head so much worrying about how to manage someone's behaviour and trying to keep it all together when he's clearly not caring or all that concerned about it. Imagine who she could become with more energetic capacity and space to focus on the positive. Imagine if she just let it go and stopped trying to make him act in the way she needed him to act. If she just let him be who he was at his core, and she just let herself be who she was at her core. And if that meant their relationship had to end, then at least they were both free to meet others who were already aligned with who they were and what they valued. I think this a lot when I meet many couples in a social setting. Imagine where they would be in themselves if they stopped trying to hold on and control.

67

SHIFTING FROM A HUMAN, EGO-LED LIFE TO A SOUL-LED LIFE

Leaving my marriage came with so much undoing of my past life and a walking away from it. The selling of the house. The splitting of the possessions. Losing of some friendships. Even my identity changing. It felt like I chose myself and then lost so much of what I loved in the process. Earlier, I talked about the three types of people we encounter during the finding love after divorce journey. The third being the awake human who is leading and living entirely from the point of their soul. Their physical world and relationships are built around them in such a way that it supports their soul and its growth. This person is living in alignment with their soul and is in alignment with their twin flame even if they haven't met them yet. Whether they meet them now or whether they will meet them later in their life path, they are in growing alignment with one another. I want to let you know that this individual didn't miraculously find themselves born into such an aligned space or have it magically appear. They purposefully created this aligned life over time. And that purposeful creation required them to, at many different times, let go of the elements, relationships and parts of their life that were no longer in alignment with their soul and who they were becoming.

Making big changes has felt harder and clunkier the older I get. Including those times when I wanted and asked for the change. During those moments, the physical world around me felt binding; the weight of change felt heavy. And internally, my thinking, beliefs about myself and concept of right for me and no longer meant for me was shifting. There were mortgages to consider. Children to consider. My living situation to consider. What sort of work I wanted to do now (and if I was even going to be able to do it well). Affordability and finances to consider. Relationships to consider. Responsibilities to weigh up. All of these things weighed heavily on me at different points in my journey of changing my life to be one that was soul-led and in alignment with who I really was.

Your own awakening process will happen for you. How far you choose to travel down the path of realigning your life to be more soul-led will be your own personal journey. However, you choose to walk it, this process always begins with one step. To just start. Start with your greatest source of pain and frustration in your life and work to create change and evolve forward in that space first. And then begin to slowly start stripping back more and more of the elements of your life that are not in alignment. If your job is sucking the life force out of you, then what could you do instead? If your financial fear is limiting your future choices, then what action can you take to open and improve your mindset? If the place or city you are living in creates financial stress, then do you need to be living there? Is your romantic relationship aligned with what you value and how you feel? Undoing the physical human ties that bind and keep us trapped and limited from ascending is a life-long process for many.

It's not a race. But it is a place that, once arrived, you can never go back. A place where your world and relationships are in alignment with what your soul desires. This is why you hear divorced people look at not-so-happily married couples and wonder why and how they are still doing it to themselves.

Once you've ascended out of such a limitation in your intimate relationship, you find yourself too awake to return back to anything less than what is now your new normal. I don't want to glorify this.

It can be a contrasting journey of both love and loss. This path is not always an easy one to walk. It can be extremely uncomfortable and triggering at points. But it is a path that, once walked, you never look back on with regret. You are free in many senses of the word. You have left the trap that many around you are still living in and trying to make work. You are free to create a life and love that is meant for you, aligned for you and that is a reflection of who you are now.

68

CHOOSING TO IGNORE THE SOUL JOURNEY WITHIN

For most of us, our outer world does not support the soul within. This is a sad reflection of modern society and everything we have valued or been taught to value and prioritise in life. We repeat the same tasks today that we did yesterday, we swipe and seek connection or entertainment, we sacrifice ourselves to keep everyone else happy or our finances together, we share our bed and our body, our most intimate space, with someone who doesn't even treat us well, we desire to look a certain way, so we feel good enough to others. You can choose to ignore the inner soul journey as much as you like, but the consequences of doing so will continue to follow you for as long as you do so. Inner turmoil. A feeling of disconnect. Confusion. A strong intuition that something feels wrong. Depression. Carrying excess weight. Sleeplessness. These are the rumblings of a soul that is desiring to be heard. When we ignore our soul desire for too long, we go on to experience the age-old mid-life crisis. A mid-life crisis is someone re-aligning their human life to their soul. A mid-life crisis is someone beginning to listen to the soul journey within without even realising that they are. The individual who walks away from everything they once loved. Who quits their job. Sells everything up. Buys a motorbike. What are they doing? Who are they? They are free, is what they are. Specifically, their soul has started to speak and has taken over the reins of their life. This person feels liberated. Free. They feel happier and lighter than they've felt in a very long time. They feel younger. And they often look it too. The weight on our psyche when we ignore the soul journey within is a heavy one.

You won't realise it until you drop the human load and start to live and make choices from a soul place. This is not a shirking of your responsibilities. It is an adjustment of them. Of course, not everyone is going to agree. Perhaps some of you here have had this happen to you, courtesy of your ex-partners. In this case, we must let them go. It's pointless to judge them or to carry too much resentment for too long. This doesn't erase your hurt or justify their behaviour. Instead, it just leaves you with acceptance. You might not agree with it. You might not have wanted it, but your ex-partners soul outgrew your connection together as it was. And they couldn't ignore their inner turmoil over it any longer.

Use this as the opportunity for you to now come into alignment with who you really are at a soul level. To reinvent and reimagine yourself for the future. To become your best version of self. It's very hard, near impossible, to find a love that is aligned for you when you are living out of alignment within yourself. Alignment and coming home to your soul is everything. It is the new version of modern-day success, to have a life that feels as good on the inside as it looks on the outside.

69
GRIEF AND LETTING GO TO MOVE ON

The death of a potential future dream is often the hardest part to let go of when a relationship ends. This feeling is further amplified when a marriage ends. No one marries hoping to one day get a divorce. No one stays in a relationship hoping it will end. The more we are aware of the death of the potential and the possibility and the grief that comes with this loss, the more we can accept and allow our feelings to simply exist. Often this grief is more about what the relationship could have been, or what we hoped it might be, than what it actually was. Fighting our emotions is futile. Especially in this space. There is a process of releasing and letting go that forms part of a relationship ending that we can't gloss over as much as we might try. It inevitably catches up with the individual later if they try to dismiss it. The same rules of grief that we apply to a loved one dying in our life can be applied to the end of a relationship. This is because it is the sudden absence of someone from your life that was once important to you. Only, they are still living which can sometimes make it harder to accept. Grief takes time.

You will find yourself missing someone's presence for a time until one day you wake up and realise that you have learnt to live without their presence in your life. And without you even realising that you'd reached this place. Your soul and psyche have accommodated their absence from your life. And just when you think you have grieved the loss of them and have moved on something will happen that will trigger you to fall back into that grief again.

Healing is not linear. Neither is grief. Grief, once resolved, eventually leaves us with memories that I hope will be ones that are later laced with gratitude for you in your soul. You cannot fight grief. Grief is an emotion that we have to allow. Healing our grief between relationships is an important part of moving on and ascending towards 'the one'. Sitting with grief is where we are forced to face our soul lessons and mistakes, however uncomfortable the process. When we try to skip and avoid this grief process, we end up carrying our baggage with us into our next relationships. Unresolved. Thus, we almost always repeat our patterns again, this time on someone else, because we haven't had the space to learn and reflect. Expect grief to come and go for quite some time after a marriage and a divorce ends. Even if you were the one who chose to walk away. Expect that just when you thought you'd overcome the loss of a person or relationship in your life, something else will happen and make you realise that you have not. Simply allow the grief and letting go process to be what it is for you. There is no timeline for grief. In fact, the grief we feel is often more of a reflection of the depth of connection we felt or amount of hope we held for the future than it is about the length of time that we were with someone. We elongate the process of moving on if we don't allow grief to be what it is for us.

70
TRUSTING THE TIMELINE OF YOUR LOVE JOURNEY

Why hasn't love happened for me yet? Where is he? Where is she? I am tired of the dating world. Tired of being on my own. I hear this a lot. There are many who feel and carry with them a distinct feeling of pain because love has not shown up for them as they hoped. Yet. Yet is the word. Remember that. It doesn't say anything negative about you if you haven't met your one yet. But it is often a reflection that something necessary at a soul level needs to take place, be completed, mastered or changed first. Almost anyone could walk outside today or put themselves on a dating app and find someone for themselves if they wanted to. That is, if you released all of your ideals, values or desires. I am not advising you to do this. I am, however, asking you to recognise that there is the potential for love everywhere in the world. And your singleness is therefore not a reflection of not being good enough.

Love finds all of us when we are walking on our soul alignment path. When we are releasing what is not meant for us and what we don't love in our lives and are instead filling our life with things meant for us that we do love. The love meant for us finds our way to us when we are becoming who we are meant to be. So, if love hasn't arrived for you yet then it is simply a case of it not being the right time for it to have walked into your life. One day, at the perfect life moment, you will walk around a corner and bump into a soul that you never expected to meet, at your new job, in the city you've just moved to, at a new friend's birthday dinner, at the club of the new hobby you've taken up. Or someone who you have never fully noticed in your life before will suddenly be someone that you do notice, and they will notice you because you've both changed, and your souls will recognise one another.

The magic of love. It shows up when you're not looking for it. When you don't need it. When you're happily living life. Keep walking your soul path. Keep becoming who you're meant to become and creating a life that reflects the essence of who you are. And when they do show up, you know as well as I do the story of how this goes. The timing of their full arrival into your life will be perfect. And you'll both be ready for one another. And with hindsight you won't want to change a single thing about the story of how it all came together for you. It will all make complete sense. Replace the pain of absence with trust in the journey, stay in soul alignment and keep having fun along the way. This is how love finds you. Release the timeline and the energy of waiting. Embrace that it will happen for you when it is supposed to. Until then, you deserve to live every moment feeling full, happy and joyous.

71

FEARING YOU WILL END UP ALONE AND NEVER FIND LOVE

When someone leaves a relationship, by choice or consequence, one of the most common fears I hear expressed is will I end up alone or will someone ever love me again? The truth is that, yes, you might be alone for a time. Yes, it might take some time for you to find someone who loves you intimately again. You might be alone for a little while. In fact, I hope you are. You might be alone for a time and if you are, you will be fine. More than fine. Rather than fearing ending up alone I'd love for you to do the opposite. I'd love for you to embrace being alone for a time. Knowing it's not forever, it's just for a time. And it means absolutely nothing negative if you don't have a partner for a period of time. It means only what you say it means. I'm on my own because I'm too old and no one wants me. I'm on my own because all men/women are (insert your favourite belief here). I'm on my own because no one wants me. None of this is actually true. It means nothing negative about anyone.

If there is one thing, I wish I'd done differently since leaving my marriage in 2016, it's that I wish I'd embraced and enjoyed being on my own more than what I did. Instead of fighting it and trying to fill the space. I wish I'd just allowed it and seen it for the gift that it was. When we fight our loneliness and try to fill the space because it's uncomfortable or triggering, we can let people slip into our life, relationships and energies that in time end up reminding us why we'd have been better off staying on our own.

Finding peace in being alone is essential to you discovering who you are. And for some of you here that is a necessary part of your soul journey. It took me five years to discover who I was, and I discovered this through time being in a relationship and through the contrast of time being on my own. Only I wasn't on my own and without love. I might not have had a partner in my life, but did I have love in my life? Yes, of course, I did. I had it everywhere. From my daughters. From my friends. From my family. From myself. From my work colleagues. Love is everywhere. Being alone is only ever a problem when we equate it to meaning something negative or less than about ourselves. And that is a BS narrative. I don't even need to know you to know that this is not true about you. You being alone does not mean you will be alone forever. You being alone for a period of time isn't something to fear. Trust your journey, please.

72

STAYING ABOVE THE CAR CRASH THAT CAN BE THE DATING POOL

You've already settled to keep love in your life before. You've already compromised for love to the detriment of yourself in the past. Decide that you have no desire to do that to yourself anymore. And don't! And be comfortable to not do so. Stay above the car crash and make the deliberate choice to not be in it. This requires you to have more of an observer's role to the dating world and process. Staying out of the car crash that is the dating world is you removing yourself from the karmic cycle of other people's lessons and choosing to learn yours in a less traumatic fashion until you meet someone worthy of your time and energy. If you are dating because you are lonely, know that you can choose to add trauma upon trauma by filling your void of loneliness with a physical body of someone else or you can go out and fill your life with people and experiences that will make your life feel fuller and more meaningful. You can be single, looking for love and not be in the car crash. It's a choice to not be in the car crash and to observe others that are.

My advice as an awakened soul is to stay above it. You will only ever set yourself back every time you dive back into it in a moment of loneliness and desperation. You can't avoid the karmic lessons that you need to have. But you can choose the way you get to learn them! Choose them kindly for yourself.

73
COMING TO LOVE FROM A PLACE OF FIX ME, SAVE ME OR MAKE ME FEEL BETTER ABOUT MYSELF

There is much that can go wrong when we come to love from a of void. Have you learnt this post-marriage? This is not to say that we can't ever come to a relationship from a place of need. Of course, we can. But. And it's a big one. If you are coming to a relationship from a place of having a person prop you up emotionally, financially, in your confidence or in any other way, then we are avoiding doing the inner work and embodying growth for ourselves; we are outsourcing and using someone else to embolden us. And the danger is that if the love from this person leaves our life, then it can deeply shake our emotional and financial stability or confidence. It leaves you again very vulnerable in a relationship because you are not coming to a relationship from a soul empowered whole place. And for many of us who have left a marriage, we have already learnt the price of coming to a relationship from a place of fix me, make me feel safe or make me feel better about myself.

The dynamic that was once the attractive hook at the start became the trap that eventually made us fear leaving the relationship. A relationship should add to us becoming the best version of ourselves possible. It is the cliché of two whole people coming together in a relationship. They are both of the energy that is love me well or leave me alone. This is a very different tone of relationship that we often see associated with the opposite energy of love me badly, but I still won't leave you. My personal and professional experience is that it will take most of us several versions of both kinds of relationships to evolve us into the space where we are ready for our twin flame.

The ultimate best version of ourselves is revealed to us through time. It is through the contrast of having poor and great relationships that realigns us onto our soul path. This happens over time, until we meet someone we won't outgrow. The invitation to meeting the one sooner is to ensure you are always coming to every relationship as whole as possible in that moment in time. Embody the energy of love me well or leave me alone. And embrace a relationship for as long as it encapsulates this energy.

74

HOLDING ONTO SOMEONE BELIEVING THEY'RE YOUR ONE

One of the most common things I see in my clients is the above. Holding onto the love and connection with a particular person despite their behaviour. We hold onto a person who has left us believing or hoping that they will come back wanting us, ready to be the person we wanted them to be, what we originally saw in them. There is no faster way to keep ourselves stuck or prevent our souls from evolving forward than to approach love from this space of holding onto someone who is no longer meant for us or good for us. I say this without judgment. I have been here myself and betrayed myself in the process. The one who got away. Walking away from someone even though you still love them. When we stop holding onto someone and start walking forward, what are we really doing? We are putting ourselves before our love for another. This is us saying to the constellations through our actions that I love myself more than I love someone else.

I love myself more. I love myself more. Just saying those words is realigning and affirming for our soul. It is an invitation to return all of our power back to ourselves, to let go and to detach from the outcome. Detachment allows the universe to create a perfect result. What is not meant to stay in your life will leave your life, regardless of how much you manipulate or twist it. When we manipulate, twist or try to create an outcome, we are choosing to delay the inevitable for another time. As one of my clients said to me when I asked her, 'If you'd been more confident in yourself in the past, when would you have left your ex-husband?' Her answer, 'Twenty-two years ago, when I first caught him out.'

Keep growing and evolving, releasing along the way what isn't aligned for you because it doesn't treat you right, feel right or because it doesn't align with the values or your soul. Sometimes the people we love so dearly wake up only once we've left them. This is their journey to walk, not yours. And it will be their journey to fix or make their way back into your life if they wake up and realise their misstep, again, not yours. And it will be your free will if you choose to go back or realise you have evolved out of the necessity for the relationship. Rarely, does someone wake up to a love lost and the changes they need to make while the love is still so readily available to them at a lower level of vibration.

Embody the energy of the love you desire to have in your life even if it is not in your life yet and keep walking your soul path that is aligned with this. The beautiful double win of approaching love and life in this way is what's meant for you will return and what is not meant for you will fall away. Either way, you will have continued further along your soul path and found yourself having evolved into something even more wonderful. When that happens, you won't look back or want to go back to how things were. You will have evolved into a whole lot more. The result will be perfect however it falls.

75
ATTACHED MORE THAN YOU ARE IN LOVE

A slippery slope that we often see in long-term relationships is where the behaviour is something we would never have accepted at the start of the relationship. As Emma Thompson, an English actress who caught her then director husband having affairs with other women on set, said, 'What I learned was how easy it is to be blinded by your own desire to deceive yourself.' Those with low levels of self-worth, self-trust and confidence, even those who also hold deep fears about leaving, will adjust their expectations, values and ideals and continue to keep doing so even as the situation becomes more uncomfortable. We all need to adjust with people and situations, but we also need to be sure when we need to move on.

If we allow people to exploit us physically, emotionally, financially, spiritually or mentally, the sad truth is that some people will continue to do so. Would I love this person in the same deep way if they showed up in my life today as a stranger and treated me how they're treating me now? If they made me feel about myself like I do now? Made me question myself like I am now? If your answer to this question is a no, then we have some soul path adjusting to do. You are more attached to how someone was in the past than you are in love with who they are now. This is dangerous territory that will cost you your soul evolution, growth and happiness if you don't allow yourself to ascend out of it.

76
EXPRESSING YOUR NEEDS AND TRUTH

Keeping the peace and not speaking our truth is a behaviour I see present in the current marriages and past marriages of many of my clients. If not from them, then from their partner or ex-partner. But typically, both have danced around these behaviours. A healthy level of compromise is always present in a relationship. However, what I see are many marriages continuing to survive and exist because one if not both are deliberately not sharing their full truth and are more intent on keeping the peace than creating real peace (which costs them their inner peace). This approach never improves a relationship. It simply enables it to continue on forward in the same manner. Learning to express our needs and our truth after we leave a marriage is a block to overcome for those who survived the constraints of their marriage by learning to bite their tongue and by learning to not express their needs and instead bottle them up.

A healthy relationship with unconditional love can embrace the expression of your needs and truth when conveyed from a place of love. This will require you to learn how to express your needs and to do so comfortably. To share and talk with honesty. To learn not to just automatically tell someone what you think they want or need to hear. Clarity and truth in a relationship allows the relationship to maintain a beautiful level of openness and connection that will not only transform and maintain your emotional connection together but also your sexual and intimate connection. Open communication, a foundation of truth and honesty and learning to express our needs are the pathway to this.

77
OVER-FOCUSING ON LOVE AND FINDING A PARTNER

I know for many of us after ending a marriage of many years that the thought of being on our own feels overwhelming, triggering and uncomfortable. We have become so used to being with someone that we can't imagine doing life on our own. And we might not want to. One of my biggest soul evolutions was when I was able to reach a point of deep recognition where I could say that if I never had another relationship in my life that I'd still have lived a full, happy life full of love and adventure. When I reached this point of evolution, what do you think happened? I stopped looking. And I got on with living a full, happy life full of love, adventure and amazingness in the present. What do you think happened then? You already know the answer because it is so obvious. I stopped looking from a place of need and from seeking love outside of myself. And I started to focus on my soul path. I found peace in aloneness. In fact, moments of aloneness became fabulous. I released all of the things and people that didn't bring peace and joy and brought into my life more of the things that did bring peace and joy. I embraced every soul lesson that I needed to have to move myself forward instead of hoping that someone would magically enter my life and save me from having to learn it. This allowed me to embody it for myself. Financially and spiritually. All of this created a deep level of contentedness and alignment in my life that brought with it a knowingness that I was on my soul path where time would bring the right person to me at the right time.

If I had focused on love, I would have done so to the detriment of myself, to my own growth and to my soul path. I would not be who

I am today. If you stop looking for love and instead throw all of your anxiety about being single into yourself, where will you be in yourself today? I would suggest much further along.

78
EMBRACING THE SEASON YOU'RE IN

One of the beautiful energies of working with a coach like myself is my ability to look at my clients and see quite clearly where their focus and attention needs to go in this moment in time. It is almost always something they don't want to or can't see for themselves. And sometimes not the area of life that an individual comes to me seeking clarity and support on. There is what we want and think we need. And then there is what we should want and actually do need to evolve us further in life and towards love.

I shared with you that when I left my marriage all I was seeking was to find love again. That was my desperate desire and soul need. And I did find love again, of course, but it was a love that I continued to keep outgrowing. And why? Because I wasn't who I was meant to be and who I was evolving into. Every relationship was a buffer for everything I was avoiding and not wanting to face within me. For me, being in my marriage took me further away from who I was not. I find this a very common scenario for the individual in the marriage who was of the softer, less dominating energy in the relationship. I morphed myself to fit into the container of the relationship and I lost myself in the process. Finding myself again was my season.

If you stopped looking for love and instead focused on the other areas of your life that needed your attention, knowing that love will find you while you are living your soul path, what can you see is the season of life that you're living right now? Is it to find yourself again? To find your feet? To thrive in your career? Feel confident in your finances and find independence? Is your life calling you to move or relocate? Un-becoming after a marriage ends, even when a long-term relationship ends, is a necessary process for some. Some are ready to dive straight back into a new relationship soon after a marriage ends because they are already living in alignment with who they already are and were meant to be. They were that person already in their marriage.

That was not my journey. My season involved coming home to me. It meant learning to express my needs and discovering what I wanted for myself as a single woman now that I no longer had a man in my life defining me and telling me what we were going to be doing or who I needed to be. It involved entirely changing my career to what it is today. Moving cities. This was something I'd been wanting to do for sixteen years prior, but that my marriage didn't allow. And there was so much more.

Please embrace the season that you're in and the necessary growth needed for that season. Resisting it doesn't change the season you're in. In fact, when we embrace it, we allow more peace to join us on the journey. We allow ourselves to walk the path with more grace and ease. What you will discover is that every lesson learnt and embodied that you pass through leads you to the next in a very straightforward manner. You can't run before you learn to walk. That old adage rings true here. You can't be further along than where you are right now until you master where you currently are. This is us taking more of a bird's-eye view to our lives where we recognise why we need to do this and that before we could ever find ourselves ready and an energetic match for our one.

Remember our fate and soul destiny never changes. All that we have control over is our free will. And our free will can either keep us on the path or take us off the path. It will speed up or hinder the ascension process. Embracing the season that you're in speeds up the ascension process to you living life as your best self where the one will eventually find you.

Happily loving life already, open-hearted and ready.

79
OVERCOMING YOUR CHILDHOOD AND ITS IMPRINT ON YOUR PSYCHE

Who were you before life and your childhood happened to you? We can have an upbringing with supportive and loving parents and still find ourselves walking into adulthood needing to undo the imprint childhood has left on the psyche. The humanness of life intruding on the soul from the moment we leave the womb. We go from a warm environment of peace, muffled noise and nurturing to noise, bright lights, a stranger's touch, pricks on the heels to be jabbed and injected with this and that, and now having to work for our food, love, attention and affection. No wonder most of us come into the world screaming and crying. If we were born into an abusive environment then we can definitely look to our parents and wish they'd been better, more evolved and loving parents. For better or worse, with all that they knew, your parents did the best that they could with you. As adults, most of us can say this with love in our hearts towards our parents.

Overcoming our childhood is us realigning ourselves with our soul path, before life and the world happened to us. Shaping us to become who we thought we needed to become. To survive. To receive love. Sometimes who we became as the result of our childhood and the patterns and behaviours we took on are not a reflection of who we actually are on the inside. It might, for instance, support the dynamics and needs of the family unit, but actually, if we reflect a little, it might not have fully supported who you were then or even now. Your role as an individual that you took on within the family and carried into adulthood for yourself may be holding you back and impacting your path today as an adult.

The best example I can share with you here is myself. I am the eldest of three children. My mum was nineteen when she had me. And I later went on to be the eldest of four children. My mum re-partnered when I was fifteen and had my half-sister. As the eldest and only girl with two younger brothers for the early years of my life, I took on the role of the responsible one. I helped Mum a lot. I helped my brothers. I learnt how to read between the lines of what someone needed and the emotions of my home because emotions weren't always communicated. When my parents fought, they gave each other the silent treatment for days. They liked to break the ice by going to a friend's place for coffee. We'd drive to their friend's house with neither of my parents talking in the car and we'd drive home with them acting mostly normal again.

As a child, I made the smart, right and good decisions. And I didn't miss a thing that my parents tried to hide or thought they were doing a good job of hiding. I became a perfectionist, the natural over-achiever in school and sport, I won every running race. Made state teams. Always got As on my tests. And my family and friends began to expect it of me. I started to identify and expect it from myself. Anything less than first was a failure for me. I became so hard on myself that I transferred it onto all of the other areas of my life and at fourteen, I was hospitalised into an adult mental health institution where I stayed for six months with anorexia. At 5'9, I weighed 30 kilograms. If I was going to have anorexia, even then I was going to make sure that I did that well too. Such was the perfectionist mindset. A+ at being an anorexic. But why did I do this to myself? Because underneath the role that I took on as the eldest child, responsible, high achieving, smart daughter who strived and thrived, who was serious and helped everyone, I was actually someone else in my soul. I was highly sensitive, perceptive, empathetic and deeply intuitive. I was creative. I was silly, sweet and fun.

I was shy. My childhood and my family role, accidentally, did not support my soul. I overcame anorexia but battled with depression and obsessive-compulsive disorder for many years after. From the moment of recovering from anorexia I literally let go and I stopped trying and pushing myself so hard. I released all need to be the best. I stopped all competitive sports. I settled for Bs and whatever else in my grades. And because I'd come so close to killing myself because of my striving, no one in my social circle or family ever brought up my lower grades or the disappearance of my competitive nature. There's no louder message than to sit in front of your loved ones as a skeletal form to let them know *I'm not happy and this isn't working for me*, and for them to adjust their parameters and expectations for you as result …

However, I continued to hold onto the role of the responsible one in the family. I lost all attachment to needing to achieve. I went to the University of Melbourne on a full scholarship that I somehow managed to attain for myself without applying for it. I went from over-achiever to someone who kept having things fall into place for her without too much effort. I chose for myself a smart job as a dental hygienist. I chose the profession solely based on the income I knew I'd earn once I graduated. I ignored my creativity. I ignored my natural ability to read and see through people and their behaviours. I ignored my inbuilt desire to connect with and help people. I chose my marriage from the place of being who I thought I needed to be, a success in life and to receive love. He was smart, attractive, a good choice on many levels. Though I didn't recognise it at the time, for me, leaving my marriage freed me to be who I really was. I just felt so free. I find this to be true for many men and women after their marriages end.

Leaving a marriage opens allows someone to recalibrate their values, their life direction, even their sense of purpose that their marriage didn't permit. I lived for thirty-five years as one version of self that the human world had propelled me to take on, over and above my soul desires. It took me the next five years after that to undo the thirty-five years before to reach a point where my life was designed around and supporting my soul in my relationships, friendships, career and lifestyle. My invitation to you here as you explore the imprint that your childhood has had on your psyche and on your choices is to find for yourself a picture of you as a child. You at an age where you were beautifully innocent and completely you before the world began to change and shape you into who you needed to be. Putting shields around your heart. Taking on a role. Closing your voice out of safety or so you weren't seen as this or that. Who were you? What did you love doing? What words would you use to describe yourself then? If you hadn't had the family dynamic you did, who else could you have become? I'd like to suggest that underneath your adultness you still have that same soul energy and essence today that you had as a child. It's just hidden under layers of responsibility, people pleasing, self-abandonment, fear, striving for success, or whatever else. My request is that you start becoming and taking on the energy of the words that landed on your heart when you looked at the photo of yourself as a child.

That is who you are underneath it all, and the sooner we can have you as an adult, living from this essence, the sooner we will have you again on your soul path. Who you always were before the world happened to you.

80
WHEN YOU KEEP ATTRACTING A TYPE

This chapter could also be called Why You Keep Pursuing A Type. Because it's never solely a question of who or what we attract. We attract all sorts of people into our everyday world. It's who we choose from within what we attract that speaks volumes. And it says as much about us as it does them. It's a hard truth to swallow.

The lessons never come from labelling someone. The lesson always comes when we reflect back on ourselves. This never means we are at fault or the cause of another's behaviour. But we do have to own that we were at one time attracted to them and to our past lovers and partners. Our personality helped enable them to some degree. Understanding the 'why' to that question reveals everything about us and our inner workings.

If you are:
- Meeting and attracting the same kinds of partners on repeat.
- Having continually bad dating experiences.
- Finding it difficult to trust, be vulnerable and find yourself expecting the worst or seeing the worst in the opposite sex.

Then we haven't dug deep enough on this why and healed the parts of ourselves that need love and attention. There is something even deeper than we realise that is shaping our choices and perceptions. This is a life hurdle to overcome on your path to finding the one that many of us have to face at one point in time. Many of us spend too much time analysing the toxic, emotionally unavailable, narcissistic person and not enough time asking, 'why were they attracted to me?' or 'why did they think they could even try it on with me?'

We are never to blame for the way someone has treated us. We never asked for it. This is not us shaming ourselves either. But there was something about you that attracted them to you. They have a type too. And it was you.

81

PUTTING YOUR DESIRE FOR A CONNECTION WITH SOMEONE ELSE ABOVE YOUR LOVE FOR SELF

There are things we do for love and to keep love in our lives, sometimes to the point of self-ruin and self-sacrifice. I see many men and women embodying the opposite of love me well or leave me alone. Instead, their energy and behaviour says love me badly and I still won't leave you. It's a dangerous dynamic that we create and perpetuate when we allow someone to treat us in a way that is less than how we deserve. When compounded over years within a marriage because we signed on for a lifetime, you can see why many marriages are what they are today.

As you know, I am not anti-marriage or long-term relationships. I also don't believe that there is no room for mistakes in marriages or long-term relationships either. Of course, there are. But the energy of love me well or leave me alone says, to me, I'll bring you my best self, knowing you are bringing me your best self. It's a reflection of our self-worth. Of growth. Of a desire to keep growing and loving with one another. A recipe for honesty and emotional maturity.

Love me badly and I still won't leave you. If you are carrying yourself with this energy, then you won't make anyone rise up in love or allow them to leave your life so you can find someone who will. In fact, you might even fight and resist them ever leaving you. Love me well or leave me alone. No relationship should make you self-compromise to a point of less than what you deserve. It is your beliefs about yourself and around the availability of love in your life that are stopping you from owning this energy.

82

LETTING GO OF A LOVE THAT HAS COME TO AN END IN YOUR LIFE

One of the hardest things we can do on our love journey is to let go of someone in our life and to release them from our head because we know that our love has come to an end. Grieving the loss of someone who is still alive and maybe not missing us like we are them is emotionally devastating. But this is necessary work on the path to finding our one. We must let go of love that we've outgrown because it's no longer meant for us or because it isn't treating us like we deserve. I always ask my clients to view moments like this from several points of perspective. Let go of any potential future presence of this person in your life.

Let go of it all. The potential future dream. How they might wake up to themselves if you just stay around and make yourself available. Instead, embrace what they have given to you in your life and what they graced you with fully accepting that this is all they are capable of giving you right now. Perhaps you have hope that someone will return to you one day.

I want you to realise this, in life we never want to go backwards. So, even if they do make a reappearance into your future, we cannot want them back in our life as the same version of who they were, just as you cannot be exactly who you were. This relationship ended for a reason. If they come back into your life as the same person with the same dynamic, you will only end again. Why go through the exact same dynamics again, having the same arguments or disappointments only to find yourself with the same result? It is naivety to expect a different result with the same personality, patterns and behaviours. No, if they return back in your future, both of you will need to be slightly different, more evolved versions of yourselves than you were previously for the relationship to be better. Both of you will have needed to have woken up to something and evolved as a result of it.

We never go backwards on our soul life path. We are either repeating the same patterns and lessons again and again until we learn them, or we are moving forward. Let go of that person and of that version of your love together. Be grateful for what it has shown you and stay open. Open not to a particular person, but to the type of love you desire to experience next—whoever might walk into your life or back into your life and be the person who provides it for you.

83

MANAGING MANIPULATIVE EXES WHO CONTINUE TO TRIGGER YOU AND IMPACT YOUR LIFE

Have you woken up to the realisation that leaving a controlling, emotionally manipulative partner doesn't necessarily bring an end to that dynamic? You've left the relationship but here you still are. Still dealing with the same BS from them. Maybe even worse than when you were together. I want you to know that this situation is going to more than likely be an ongoing situation for you to manage. Sadly, the only full relief that you may ever experience from it (or at least close to) is going to be when you have a new partner who is fully present in your life and whom you live with. Your ex will continue to be an ongoing reminder that at one point in your life you didn't express your needs, your boundaries, and your self-love and sense of self-worth weren't quite what they should have been. And they will continue be the presence and lesson of a reminder that you need to embody and master this element within you as part of your soul journey. We have to manage this scenario in our lives knowing that we can control only ourselves and our self-growth. And by doing so, we can help bring out more of the positive or negative aspects within a person.

WE MUST TAKE FULL OWNERSHIP OF THE SITUATION WE ARE IN.

At some point in the past this person was attractive to us, and we were attractive to them. If they are controlling, arrogant and manipulative now, then they certainly were, even if in just little ways, in those early days when you met. Yes, they might have worsened over the years but if we look critically at ourselves there was almost always evidence of this behaviour at the start. We just chose to overlook it. I liken this to the bully in the playground scenario to help us understand. The bully knows how to pick out the other child in the playground who he can push around and try it on with. He can pick up on the energy of the child who maybe isn't all that confident, who is having a less-than-ideal or nurturing time at home. He does all of this without realising. We know this phenomenon to be true because so often if you move the child who is being bullied out of one school and place him into another school what happens? They are bullied again only in a different environment.

How is this relevant to this situation? We must own what once made us attractive to a person who likes to be in control, be dominant and will manipulate to get their own way and to remain dominant and in control. And we must do the deep inner work to resolve all of what asking that reflection reveals about us. The lacks and the voids and the beliefs we held about ourselves that their personality made up for at that time. All the facets that we're now paying for.

BE LIKE A GREY ROCK.

When we are in a conversation or situation with someone who is trying to trigger us emotionally so that we doubt ourselves, stay the same or feel inferior (enter your own personal situation here, but this person often has a superiority complex), I always ask my clients to be like a grey rock. Be bland with your answers. Let your answers be even tempered, cool, calm and collected and not reactive. Present the facts and don't colour or embellish or add emotive language to the situation when you're in conversation. Be as boring as you can be with your replies and don't bite. However they react, stay in the same vibration of being a boring, grey rock. Understand that this person is often naturally more combative than you are. They probably even get a bit of a rise out of it all. So don't even try to out-win them in this arena. Refuse to participate in it. Know your worth. Hold your ground. Stay true to the outcome or intention you hold for the situation. Be a grey rock.

RECOMMIT TO YOURSELF.

I made a commitment to myself when I left Perth that I was never again going to tolerate emotionally manipulative or controlling behaviour from anyone in my life ever again. I'd already drawn a line under it but this was the firmest, hardest line that I'd ever drawn in my mind. It was an absolute, I'm-not-buying-in-to-it-anymore decision. There's a difference in drawing a line in the sand and drawing an absolute line in concrete. This recommitment is going to be important for you into the future. Because if you have children with an ex-partner who is bringing this dynamic into your life when they are triggered, then know that you are more than likely going to experience future reoccurrences of this dynamic whenever they see fit. When you are progressing or moving forward in your life, doing something they don't agree with or want. If they feel they are losing control or superiority over you or the situation.

This situation is going to take a lot of resilience, confidence and a sense of empowerment greater than you potentially hold now. I want you know that you can eclipse this dynamic and rise above it. And rise above it again when you need to in the future. It will take skills that you might not have now and a vision for your future grander than you have possibly created for yourself in this moment. But this is the pathway to rising above it.

We should never allow ourselves to be pushed around emotionally by bullies, whether we are in the playground as a child or elsewhere as adults. Ultimately, it is us who decides when we will no longer tolerate it. When we draw a line of 'no more' on it. When we decide to stop tip-toeing around or trying to keep the peace with someone who is intent on bullying and manipulating us.

> ***PLEASE NOTE:** I don't apply this advice to situations of domestic violence. Please seek professional support for yourself in this environment.*

84

SITUATIONSHIPS AND NON-COMMITTAL LOVERS: WHAT TO DO WITH THEM

If you are genuinely happy with the relationship status of a situationship, by all means, stay there. But if you know in your heart that you're only there because you're hoping they will one day want a committed relationship, then we must stop lying to ourselves and stand firm in our truth. The greater the disconnect between what you truly want and what you are accepting, the more shame and lack of self-love you are building within yourself. If someone has confirmed that they don't want a relationship through their words or actions, and yet you keep jumping through hoops to be available to them or to please them hoping they will change for you, then you are being toxic to yourself. If you are dissatisfied with what you are getting in love and life, then you are responsible for changing that. You can either honour and respect yourself and walk away from hot-cold, on-off dynamics, or you can continue hoping that your love will change the other person if you just keep hanging around.

Truth. People change when they want to, not when you want them to. People are ready for a relationship when they are, not when you need them to be. It is their own desire, willingness and commitment towards change that changes them. And it could also be a reflection of how much they love and desire you. Even if you are coming from a manipulative place, over-extending yourself and over functioning to keep the connection in your life it is actually the worst strategy that you could utilise to convert the other person into wanting you. The chances of someone committing to you by you staying involved in a situationship with them is close to zero. When they can have their cake and eat it too, what is the incentive for them to change? How will they miss you? See your full worth? If there's anything that would inspire a change of heart with someone, it would be the realisation that they risk losing you if they are unwilling to offer a relationship if that is what you seek. Walk away from them, not because you want to manipulate them into wanting you but because you don't want to be in a misaligned connection that is born out of self-abandonment.

If you want a committed relationship, then honour that desire. You deserve it.

85
AFFAIRS AND THIRD-PARTY SITUATIONS

An affair often wakes you up in such a way that you can't go back to sleep. I have no judgement towards anyone who has had an affair. I can't. Many clients of mine were the individual who had an affair in their marriage. Just as many of my clients have experienced their spouse having an affair which ultimately ended their relationship. I hear the pain, impact and turmoil that the presence of a third party has on everyone involved. Therefore, I can't have judgement. The stereotype of men being the one to have more affairs is no longer true in this age. Not everyone who had an affair is a horrible or selfish person. Not everyone is moving forward thinking only with their libido. I am not defending them. I believe affairs are wrong and unkind to the other people in the relationship. I believe them to be very wrong if you have an affair and are not honest and authentic with your partner about it. Horribly wrong if they are suspicious of a third-party presence in your relationship and to smooth things over you are downplaying their suspicion and intuition to hide your truth and behaviour. That is cruel behaviour that no one deserves. To make someone doubt and question themselves and their intuition destroys a person's confidence and sense of self-trust. And you don't give them the opportunity to steer forward their own life, on their terms. You are interfering in their life path by withholding the full truth from them, deciding for them what they need to know or would benefit from knowing.

I know that my views on affairs might be hard to accept for those here who have been cheated on, who feel abandoned or wronged. I ask you to see this from my perspective. I am privy to both sides of the story, often in more depth and having heard more honesty about people's truth and feelings than was ever expressed to their partner (usually as a way to avoid further hurting their partners or causing a bigger fallout). This is not me justifying an affair or defending anyone. I'm simply acknowledging that, for some, the affair is the soul's wakeup call that some need to have. My personal values on relationships are always based on honesty and truth and I believe this should be the case for every relationship. As soon as full honesty and transparency leaves a relationship, however someone tries to repair it or gloss over it, you have created discord in the relationship. Someone needs to shut down their intuition and not listen to it for the relationship to continue without discord. People have affairs because their relationship is no longer meeting all of their needs, because it is no longer a reflection of who they are now or who they desire to be. And people have affairs because they've overstayed in a relationship that doesn't meet their needs.

An affair wakes someone up to what they are missing and needing in an intimate relationship, whether it is an emotional or physical affair. These are often needs that an individual has been downplaying, abandoning and ignoring as necessary for their soul before the affair. An affair doesn't have to be the end of your relationship if it's approached and talked about with transparency and full honesty from all parties. But it should be the opportunity for honesty and to reflect on what needs to change in the relationship. And if that change can even happen in this relationship. Certainly, if you have been the victim of an affair or a third-party situation, I want you to know this, and as challenging an ask that this might be for you, please don't take an affair or their choice of person they had an affair with personally. It is a reflection of their unmet needs that they were trying to meet and fulfil in another person. It is not a reflection of your shortcomings in any way. They outgrew you. Perhaps for many years they could feel this happening and were trying to fight their feelings and continued to show up in the relationship because they did love and care for you, until one day they couldn't any longer. We will never fully know.

What I hear over and over from those who have had an affair is: I'm not this person. I never meant for this to happen. I feel so guilty. What do I do now because I can't go back to how things were? There are always two sides to every coin. And while we can judge someone harshly for doing what they've done and for ending a relationship in this way, what I do wish for your soul? For you to not carry this forward in your heart and make it anything about you. Instead, I'd like you to reflect and think I wish they'd had the courage to tell me that they were unhappy and weren't sure if they still wanted to be here with me for me. Not here because of our children and the home we'd built together. Regardless of everything, I wish they'd had the courage to be honest.

Because all of us deserve to be in a relationship with someone who wants to be fully with us. For someone to be with us because they love us, not because they feel obliged to be with us or fear the financial, personal, or social fallout consequences of leaving us. That's not love. For many, that's marriage.

86
ATTACHING TO NEW LOVE FAST

Is this you? This almost always occurs due to a perceived belief of their being a lack of love in the world for you. Finally, someone sees you and makes you feel appreciated. Offers love, affection and attention. We are hooked in with how it makes us feel about ourselves, we are excited by the potential we see in them, even though we don't really know them yet. We are attached. We haven't even begun to fully know the individual. All of their personalities and qualities. Their children and family dynamics. Allowing love and a connection to grow slowly with someone is one of life's joys. A process of revealing yourself to someone over time and them to you. Magic upon magic that, with the right person, builds into a magnetic crescendo of attraction and connection with another. The energy is magnetic when we don't rush in and instead simply allow the process to unfold naturally in due course. The energy becomes like an addiction when do you rush in. For good, bad or healthy, we're attached and hooked in. Blind to whether someone is aligned with our soul or not. My biggest desire is for you to allow the time and space to let someone reveal themselves to you. Without any future thinking, imagining or projecting from you. Simply you in the now, enjoying the process of getting to know someone in the now. Seeing them for who they are now.

I always ask my clients to allow three months to get to know a person as a mature adult. For all their nuances, desires and baggage. We all have these attributes! Date as though love is everywhere around you, because it is. Date as though you deserve only the best, because you do. You have the power to choose who you love and attach too through the power and observance of your thoughts. Ask yourself: are you imagining too far ahead with this person after only one or two dates? (Even if it is amazing.) Because you can very much desire to see a person again without being attached and pinning all your future dreams on to them as I see so many do. I would love for you to date from a place of who you want to be with over who wants to be with you. This is a very impactful, energetic shift that will raise your vibration from one of neediness to one of enjoying getting to know a person. Love does not rush. Only people do.

87

WHEN YOUR HEART HAS BEEN BROKEN TOO MANY TIMES

When we leave a marriage there are three pathways a soul will take. There is the pathway where someone has no desire to change or grow, so they will dive straight into their next relationship. One that tends to be a shade of the same. There is the pathway where someone is already in alignment with themselves, they know themselves well, they can also find themselves back in a relationship again relatively quickly. One that now matches their alignment and values. Or there is the pathway where someone is quite out of alignment with themselves. They have not been living at their fullest expression or potential in the relationship and so their journey is to grow, to find themselves and to step into their fullest potential and expression. To find their alignment. This latter person can often be left feeling like the journey to find love is more of a battle to walk. They learn who they are and what they need now through the contrast of good and bad love and life experiences after leaving a marriage. They love only to outgrow because they are ascending in different ways all the time. I know this person because I was this person.

When your heart has been hurt or disappointed too many times, I ask, please don't close, please just rest. Please just take time out. Please don't close your heart. Take time to nurture you, not from a wounded space but from a place of self-care. There is nothing in life worth closing our heart over. Choosing to live with an open heart, no matter what life throws at us, is the ultimate self-mastery. And the only way we do this is to make the deliberate decision to not close and to stay open. Do not let anything in life be wounding enough that you close your heart over it. You can either close because you don't like what happened or you can choose to keep feeling love, hope, trust and enthusiasm despite it all. Closing our heart does not really protect us from anything. Closing our hearts only serves to block us from being open to the things we actually desire to come in, which are love, connection, joy and enthusiasm.

Defining what we need to have in our life or what needs to show up in our life to be open in our hearts only limits us. We either open to all that life brings us despite it all, or we close to what life brings us. I ask, please remain open to it all. And choose to open to it again as soon as you can. One day you will reach the space where you have entirely fallen out of the habit of closing your heart to protect yourself. You are open and don't even realise that you are. Watch your energy and life path shift to one of expansion as you continue to do this. Just keep opening and opening again and not closing.

88
FEARING VULNERABILITY

How do you stay open to love when you've been hurt before? It takes tremendous courage to love with an open heart and to risk being hurt again. It's one of the scariest things we must move through after heartbreak. We have to be willing to open ourselves to someone again. To allow them a place in our heart and in our world while knowing that they might leave us, hurt us or disappoint us along the way. But what's the alternative of not being vulnerable and open-hearted? To live life with a closed heart? To be emotionally unavailable, detached or closed to love? Never trusting again or never letting anyone in again for fear that you'll get hurt? That, to me, is like having a car accident and then never driving again just in case you have another car accident one day.

Being vulnerable doesn't mean having zero boundaries. You can protect your heart while still remaining open, while still being cautious and highly selective about who you allow to take residence in your heart. But boundaries are not armour. If you recognise now that you perhaps have more armour on than you have healthy boundaries, then this is something to heal on your soul path. Loving another and allowing another to fully love us requires us to have armour and shields down. This is how we open up to true intimacy. As one of my clients said to me, 'I knew I had things backwards when I'd already had sex with him but was too shy and hesitant to reach out and hold his hand when we were walking the next day. Somehow reaching out to hold hands felt more intimate.' Reflect on this for a moment.

89
IGNORING YOUR INTUITION TO STAY IN A RELATIONSHIP

Your intuition is your soul's magical power. The inner knowing that doesn't always make sense but knows. The sixth sense all of us have. I hear this regularly from my clients when they are sharing with me the dynamics of their marriage, whether they're still in it or whether they've left.

- I knew something was going on. I suspected.
- I knew we shouldn't have married before we were married.
- They always turned it around on me like I was overthinking, anxious, reading too much into things. As though I was the problem.
- I started to believe I was insecure.
- It never felt right or added up to me and I couldn't ever let it go in my head or with him.
- I ignored my intuition. I listened to them more than I listened to myself.

Truth. No amount of gaslighting, emotional manipulation, control, attempts to forget or smoothing things over will shut down a person's intuition once it's been sparked. Someone might try to ignore their intuition by choice or through persuasion, perhaps for many years to avoid the consequences of actually listening to it. But once that antenna is on, it's on. And it will take only the slightest things in the future to flag it again and remind them. The price an individual pays for ignoring their intuition or having their intuition downplayed as wrong when it's actually right, is high. In their loss of confidence, sense of self-worth, their sexual openness with their partner, their everything. They will close off emotionally and sexually over time as a response. When you are staying in a relationship that requires you to ignore or downplay your intuition, you are laying and have laid the blueprint for a disconnected relationship. This is why someone can arrive at their late thirties, forties and fifties, and find themselves in a relationship that their younger, less wise, less confident self created the blueprint for. One that their older more evolved self can no longer tolerate.

The soul lesson here is the importance in trusting our intuition over ignoring it. Even if we don't know what has flagged our intuition exactly, simply admitting to ourselves that it is on and we don't know why is an important acknowledgement. This needs to be enough to make us stop, listen, take off the rose-coloured glasses and reflect. Our intuition is like a muscle. The more we trust it and make decisions from that place, the more the muscle grows. The more confident we are making decisions from our intuition, more than our logic.

Intuition = voice of the soul.
Logic = voice of the ego and the human mind.

And just like the dissatisfaction of the soul, intuition can't be quietened for long.

90

BECOMING AN ENERGETIC MATCH FOR YOUR IDEAL PARTNER

What do you desire in a partner now? As I've dated and left long-term relationships since my divorce, my ideal partner has changed. Things I believed were important that I needed in someone turned out to be not so important. And things that I thought weren't, all of a sudden became absolute non-negotiables. I always ask my clients when they are open to love to write down a list of ideal qualities that they would love to have in a partner. We look at the physical attributes, the personality traits, children, family attitudes and lifestyle to really create a picture of how this person moves through the world and how they love. And then I ask them this: Who would your ideal partner be attracted to? What is their type? Knowing what we want in an ideal partner is a clarifying exercise and powerful manifesting technique but only if we come to it from a place of asking if we are an energetic match for them also.

Like attracts like. Would they be attracted to us as we exist today? Someone who is health conscious and exercises four to five times a week is more than likely also going to be attracted to a health-conscious person. Someone who loves to be social and who enjoys the night life isn't going to be necessarily aligned with someone who never wants to go out. I know this to be true for me. I very rarely drink. I actually can't remember the last time I was drunk or had a hangover. It was that many years ago. And so, I could never be in a relationship with someone who spent regular weekends hungover on the couch or smelling like alcohol next to me in bed. This is no judgement to them or anyone who does this, it's merely a reflection of my values and ideal qualities in a person.

Sometimes the pathway to being in alignment so we run into and meet our ideal partner looks like us realising that if I like this type of characteristic in a person then maybe I need to embody even more of this in myself—in my energy, in my behaviour, in how I live my life. This is us co-creating and becoming our own best version of self. Which is also our ideal partner's ideal partner. Some questions for you to ponder: Am I this person already? Or am I waiting for their entry into my life to become this person?

91

FOR THOSE WHO ARE MORE COMFORTABLE GIVING LOVE THAN RECEIVING IT

Over-givers attract takers. And takers attract givers. Like two pieces of a puzzle that fit together perfectly. Notice how someone who loves to take more than they love to give never finds themselves in a relationship with someone who is also a taker? Why would they? For them there would be nothing attractive about that dynamic at all. Two takers in a relationship would butt heads, neither would feel loved, both claiming the other was selfish. A taker feels loved and nurtured when someone over-gives to them. An over-giver believes they have to over-give to be loved. See how perfectly these two fits together? Both of these individuals more than likely learnt this way of loving from their parents during childhood. Maybe they watched one over-giving and loving the other in this way and have carried forth the behaviour into adulthood. Perhaps the taker was over-nurtured in their childhood by a parent, so this now forms their expectation of what love looks like.

If you are an over-giver then you probably feel exhausted and like no one gives to you. The cure? Stop over-giving. Recognise that love also looks like receiving love and nurturing from others. I'd love for you to start expecting this. Not because you're needy but because you're worthy of receiving love. And just like someone who is uncomfortable receiving compliments needs to learn to accept compliments comfortably without brushing them off, so do you need to learn to start receiving love by allowing space for it and accepting it when it is given to you.

You do not have to over-give to the point of self-sacrifice to be loved or to keep love in your life. This is not love. This is your conditioning, and it is a karmic lesson of self-love and self-worth for you to evolve past.

92

PEOPLE-PLEASING AND THE DESIRE TO PLEASE

A marriage ending is often the death of the people-pleaser. It's the death of conformity. Of tolerating mediocrity. Of being who others needed you to be. And you're wondering why it felt so hard to decide to leave your marriage and to have the courage to own it? An important reflection to see here is that people-pleasing adults were first people-pleasing children. Every time. People-pleasing isn't inherently negative. All of us desire to please our loved ones. You might go out of your way to do things for the people in your life based on what you assume they want or need. You give up your time and energy to get them to like you. But people-pleasing generally goes beyond simple kindness. It often involves changing or altering words, behaviours and our needs for the sake of another person's feelings or reactions or to keep them in our life.

This is how people-pleasing can cause trouble in our relationships. It becomes assumed that we will always put others before ourselves. We begin to feel unappreciated and taken advantage of. People-pleasers often deal with low self-worth and draw their self-worth by gaining approval and a sense of belonging from others. They desire others to like them and fear being rejected or ostracised for putting their needs above the needs of others first. People-pleasers tend to have very little spare time because they are giving to everyone else in their lives in their spare time. Importantly, on our path to finding our one, we have to realise that our tendency to people-please will almost always attract into our life relationships that are not satisfying and that take advantage of us rather than celebrate us. Practising putting yourself first and having boundaries and saying no is how we slowly begin to overcome our people-pleasing tendencies. This almost always feels uncomfortable first because behaving in this way triggers our fears of belonging and of possible rejection.

Allow yourself to slowly expand into the energy of pleasing yourself first before others. Allow others to adjust to the new you who is beginning to say no, particularly if others are used to you always saying yes and dropping everything for them. At first this might all feel selfish to you, but trust me when I say this, if you are a people-pleaser what you deem selfish is usually far from it.

93
WE ALL DESERVE LOVE BUT SOME OF US ARE LESS READY THAN WE REALISE

I talk to a lot of people who meet emotionally unavailable people. What many people don't see however is their own emotional unavailability playing out in the story. I wonder if you were completely open to love and ready to let someone into your life, you would have been attracted to them? Most times if we look at an emotionally unavailable partner, we can see the ways in which their reluctance for a fully committed relationship in some ways kind of suited us and our lifestyle. Perhaps we were more hesitant about love than we realised. We feared rejection and vulnerability still. Perhaps we were in the season of enjoying our independence and freedom. Maybe we had very little spare time or energy left to truly offer a partner. All I know is this because I see it time and time again, the more emotionally ready and open you are to love and being in a relationship, the less attractive emotionally unavailable people become to you. Their emotional unavailability and inconsistency becomes boring. It becomes not enough. It becomes hurtful and disappointing. You lose interest over trying to keep their interest. Make sure you aren't blinded by fear and pain from the past. Recognise that you too are perhaps a little more guarded and emotionally available than you realised. And unless two emotionally unavailable people are consciously aware about their unavailability and both working to heal it then we risk you becoming even more emotionally closed and unavailable because of the nature of the relationship.

Do the healing you need to do, knowing that time doesn't heal, it's what we do with the time that heals, so that you will be able to embrace what you deserve and move on from what is not that.

94
LEADING WITH APPEARANCES

I see this regularly. We find ourselves single and one of the first things we do is turn our attention to looking good, losing weight and updating our wardrobe to attract our next partner. Being attracted to someone is essential in an intimate, loving relationship. Without that energy, you are mere friends or acquaintances. So, your looks, while not everything, are important. Your partner must be attracted to you and vice versa. However, when we lead with the way we look and our physical body as our leading asset… then both are a hindrance. Many leave a long-term relationship because one of their biggest needs is to feel desired, to feel sexy again and for someone else to see and appreciate them for it.

This is when someone starts to lead with their looks and their physical form over and above their soul and what they have to give to a person from that level. It's also the danger space where we can meet individuals who only see in us our physical looks and sex because they're leading with it too. As a result, we are going to attract those who are seeking mostly or only that. The physical skin. Sex. To be desired. How a partner looks next to them. Like attracts like. If someone is leading with their physical attributes as their best asset, then they value it first and foremost too. They're more than likely going to see that in you too.

This is why some of the most beautiful of women can end up with some of the lousiest men who don't appreciate them as souls, as people. The women have learnt through life experience that their looks were vital to their success. The drawcard. And they define themselves by their physical appearance as a result. Who do you think they attract? Men who choose them based more on their physical appearance and how they looked over genuine soul connection.

Inherently, this is two people coming from their humanness, from their ego. I want someone to value you for who you are and your soul as much as how you look. This means you have to value who you are and your soul first. You have to be in touch with this side of yourself. Let someone fall in love with that first. Let who you are be the hook that captures them. Not just how you look.

95
APPLYING RULES OF RIGHT AND WRONG TO LOVE

If love did come with a rule book, throw it out. Love has no rules. Someone will leave your life for one reason only to come back better for the time apart, now ready and knowing what they want. And someone can do the complete opposite. They leave. They wake up. They stay gone. You can be comfortably married to someone. Happily settled with your future fate and yet you connect eyes with someone unexpected and they cause an awakening and everything changes for you. There are some who might say they should never have pursued each other, or they should have handled it differently, or not done this or that but I simply want you to recognise this.

There are no rules in love. Love and connections just show up in life. Usually when we're not looking for it. Rules don't apply to love as much as we try to make them fit. When it comes to the presence of love in our life or the absence of it when someone leaves our life, we can only offer it two things: acceptance because we can't control the emotion of love in ourselves, certainly not in others; and detachment because we can't make someone love us and be ready for us when they aren't.

Love has no rules. But the journey does always make sense in the end. You never know what is right around the corner or what life is preparing you for during your soul life path. Life could be orchestrating your wildest dreams to come to fruition and it will blow you away. Stay humble, grounded and keep trusting.

96
UNDERSTANDING THE FEMININE AND MASCULINE IN LOVE

If we are to look at the masculine energy in a love relationship, what is it? The masculine exists as the container to the feminine who is held, loved and supported within it. In an ideal relationship with beautiful polarity this is the balance. The masculine is the container. The feminine exists within it. In an off-balance relationship, we can see the opposite. Instead, the feminine is the container carrying and driving the relationship. Holding it together. And the masculine exists within the container, taking an almost back seat in the relationship, keeping the peace, going with her flow more often than not. In this relationship we see the feminine person in the relationship more in her masculine energy, the one in control and often feeling resentful and tired as a result of it but feeling safe because she is in control, which is what she ultimately needs and desires. And we see the masculine person in this relationship more in his feminine energy by consequence and feeling like he has little to no freedom, slightly emasculated, slightly resentful as a result of it, but feeling cared for and nurtured. This person bites their tongue to keep the peace. They dismiss and downplay their needs.

In a less-than-trustworthy, committed energy we see this analogy of a container felt by the feminine. Her intuition picking up on the leaky energy of the container of the relationship that she is in when she feels her partner is sharing his energy or attention in anyway with other women. For the premise of your own soul journey through love there are several questions to ask ourselves here. In past relationships have you been the container or in the container? Was that aligned with your natural energy of being either feminine or masculine?

If you are the masculine energy, it is to ask ourselves: When I have been in a relationship how solid, strong and nurturing has the container been that I provided to my partner? Was it of quality? If the masculine doesn't like the results that he has received in love in the past, then this is the question he must ask himself that empowers him to love better and do better. And to choose a partner who respects the container if he knows he is producing one of quality. And if we are the feminine energy, it is to ask ourselves the opposite: In past relationships what has been the quality of container that I have placed myself in? Have they been loving, supportive, caring, nurturing and safe for me? Have I trusted it? If the feminine doesn't like the results that she has received in love in the past, then this is the question she must ask herself that empowers her to make a better choice in who she entrusts herself with. She must also acknowledge the importance of trusting her intuition if she feels the leaky energy of a container.

Generationally and culturally, we have much to do around allowing and empowering men to be in their masculine energy. Certainly, what many see as strong masculine energy today is far from what it really is at its core. Many women are also more in their masculine energy then they realise. They are the container in the relationship. Certainly, it is something I treat with almost every female client that I work with to varying degrees. Our culture of striving and success, resentment built up from carrying the energetic burden of children and relationships, and a fear of vulnerability after heartbreak or hurt shifts the feminine very quickly into a more masculine closed, protective energy. The feminine doesn't tell the masculine what to do. Instead, she gracefully influences him, often this looks like expressing her needs and holding him accountable. He can do whatever he wants. But she won't tolerate everything. In the former you sound like his mum. In the latter you are a sovereign, powerful, magnetic being. Feel the difference?

As a result of so many men not being in their masculine, strong, grounded, true to their word and in their purpose and as a result of so many women not being in their feminine, loving, nurturing, more going with the flow, soft, playful, confident, is why we are seeing such a discord in so many relationships and the dating pool today. We are absolutely seeing a rebalancing of masculine and feminine energies in relationships and within ourselves in this generational moment of time. Women expecting better quality containers of relationships to be in otherwise they will leave. Why be in something if you don't have to be and put yourself through it? The toxic, manipulative, lying and cheating behaviour is less and less accepted. Men who have done the work who need women to energetically step down and allow them to be in their masculinity and to be that container for them. The power always returning to the feminine. If you don't like the quality of the container that you find yourself in, then don't be in it.

Do you know what really weakens a man? Porn. Scrolling on socials. Prioritising making money. Video games. Drugs and alcohol. Being in a relationship with a woman who is guarded, emotionally and sexually closed and controlling also contributes further to their emasculation. A weakened man looks for a woman to lead him and give him direction because he doesn't know how to do that for himself. A strong, healthy man has boundaries, purpose, clear direction, a relationship that nourishes his masculine energy and he is grounded. Do you know what really wounds a woman? Hustle culture. Needing to feel in control. Ignoring their intuition. Replacing feelings with logic. Abandoning playfulness for seriousness. Not trusting the masculine and being in relationships where she doesn't trust him and intuitively feels his leaky energy but ignores and downplays it. A wounded woman seeks to control and curtail the freedoms of the man in her life because she fears being hurt and can feel the leaks. An at-peace relaxed sensual woman leads with her intuition and her feelings and makes her decisions from this place. She opens and shares herself where she knows she will be loved well. She is a beautiful mix of soft and strong. She is wise as much as she is playful. It will take time but as women reconnect to their feminine essence and men become more rooted in their strong masculinity, then love and relationships will heal and ascend.

This is the soul work for all of us as we look to find love and our one after divorce. For women to only place themselves in masculine containers that support them to be in their feminine and at their best essence. For men to be of the energy necessary to be these strong containers and to choose to be in relationships with women that have the awareness to nourish this in them.

97

FEELING DISHEARTENED WHILE ON THE LOVE JOURNEY

Synchronicity and divine timing is the universe's way of seducing you. Because it wants to lead you somewhere. It wants to bring you to the ultimate experience of being yourself and loving yourself. Life is more than just about whether you have a relationship in your life or not. Which doesn't mean you can't have moments of feeling disheartened or moments of wishing when will they show up. But it does mean that we must keep living and enjoying our life to the fullest in the meantime and to enjoy the process of doing everything else we were meant to experience along the way.

Synchronicity and divine timing. These are beautiful energies. They also create magical stories of love just arriving one day and walking into our life with ease, feeling like it was meant to be and at the perfect time. This will absolutely happen for you. I would like to suggest that there might be a reason why love hasn't happened for you yet. I hope this book has revealed to you something about that. What I will say is to please never allow your moments of feeling disheartened to lead you to settle or compromise in love. Always remind yourself that your life is better enjoyed when you're happily single and loving life over being in a relationship for the sake of it.

Everything you desire is out there waiting for you and all it is needing from you is for you to be living as the person that you always were underneath, you in your soul alignment. Love will struggle to find you and stay in your life when you embody the energy of someone who sits at home depressed on the couch.

Thrive in life. Work hard to be your best version of self. Trust the process. Stay grounded. Seek meaningful connections and hobbies you love. Surround yourself with good people. Expand your world and your horizons. Let the one find you. Let yourself accidentally stumble across love instead of always searching for it.

98

A BIRD'S-EYE VIEW OF YOU: WHAT IS YOUR CURRENT LIFE PATH HURDLE

I want you to take finding love off your life path for a moment. Take it completely off. We're doing this because it's not ours to put on. Love shows up when it's meant to. Love shows up when it will. Love just shows up when you're happily doing your thing. We have control over many things in our life. But not love. If we remove love from your life path, what can we see is your current life path hurdle? What can you see yourself needing to focus on or overcome right now? This is a beautiful clarifying question for us to use when we are over-focusing on the lack of relationship in our life.

As if the presence of love in our life fixes and absolves us from everything else. It does not. This is not the ideal attitude or energy to have about love. I'm not asking you to close yourself off to finding love by viewing your life path in this way. I'm asking you to instead be open to love showing up for you while you are mastering and living your life as your best version of self in the now. To be ascending in your own soul growth, healing and evolvement. Moving forward towards your one. Not standing on the spot, as the same version of self you've always been, waiting for them. What is it that you need to master and overcome in the now?

99

THE TAO: FINDING YOUR OWN INNER BALANCE AND PATH TO YOUR ALIGNMENT

The Tao. The way. The balance of the yin and the yang. The feminine and the masculine. The dark and the light. The fine balance that exists between the two extremes of cup so full and cup so empty. Let us use the example of hunger to best explain the Tao. What is the saying? A human is only nine meals away from anarchy! Imagine yourself having gone without nine straight meals over several days. Imagine how hungry you would feel (one extreme) and imagine how you would react when you were finally given food to eat. Starving so much that you would find yourself eating so quickly, overeating. Now feeling so full, satisfied but also a little uncomfortable (the other extreme). The Tao exists between both those extremes where the energies are balanced. A place of neither being so uncomfortably hungry or uncomfortably full. The way of the centre is where we find balance and where we live in harmony. When we participate and stay stuck in the extremes of anything is where we lose our way and waste our energy.

I see this in many clients after they leave a marriage. The marriage lacked sex, intimacy and attention (cup empty: extreme) so they enter into the dating world seeking connections that make them feel desired and sexy (cup full and overflowing: extreme). Individuals in this example do this dance until the extreme starts to feel lonely, tiring and no longer fulfilling. In fact, it starts to make them feel unhappy too because it lacks the one element we seek inherently—soul connection. Life begins to feel confused when we live in the place of extremes. Not because we are confused but because we're making life confusing through our behaviours. From one extreme to the other, stopping only once we let go of the extremes and allow the energy in between both to settle and find balance. The energy of balance eventually permeating and entering into our psyche and our life. When we come to love from a place of extreme, whether it is an emotional void or a sexual need, we are actually coming to love from a place of being out of balance. Sometimes we can reach this place of balance within a new relationship, which is of course ideal when we do. Sometimes it can take several relationships or situationships for us to recognise we are coming from a place of extreme and to clear it from our system.

A few things to be aware of when we are looking for love after divorce: In what way am I out of balance? What am I really seeking here? Am I in balance or out? Is what I am doing good for me in my attempts to correct my lack of balance? In what way is the individual we are dating or in a relationship with out of balance? As you centre by not participating in the extremes, this is when the energies within you will naturally find their balance.

Find your balance between the extremes and you will find yourself in growing harmony with your soul alignment. You will find yourself on your path.

100
BRINGING TO LIFE YOUR BEST SCENARIO AND NOT YOUR WORST

Almost everyone I ask can tell me their fears and their worst-case scenarios without having to give too much thought to their answer. Very few can give me their best-case scenario that they'd love to see for themselves in the next six months, one year, five years or the rest of their life with the same ease. Without realising, most of us are predominately thinking about what we don't want and what we fear more than what we do want. No wonder you are co-creating and manifesting into your life everything you don't want and not what you do want. Look at all that you're focusing on! When I can switch my clients' thought process to be predominantly focused on their best scenario without attachment to a particular person, place or thing instead of their worst scenario is when we create magic in their lives. We focus on what we do want. We release our attachment to certain people needing to be the person to instrument our best-case scenarios coming to life. We place ourselves on the path of finding our soul alignment and we let everything that is an energetic match to our best-case scenario come to us and we let everything fall away that is not.

The best scenario for ourselves becomes the intention. It is a powerful practice and manifesting technique. Try it. Write your best scenario down. Vision board it if you desire. Visit it regularly as a reminder every time you feel waylaid or find your thinking is trying to lead you back to the safety and comfort of expecting the worst. Expecting and thinking about the worst-case scenario is a habit. Change the habit. Prepare for the best to walk into your life instead.

101
WHAT DOES THIS PERSON BRING OUT IN ME, THE BEST AND THE WORST

We can love someone deeply and they can still not be good for us. Freedom and peace is accepting someone for who they are and not needing them to be anyone else, or any different to who they are now. Freedom and peace is also not fighting someone on this and releasing yourself from a situation that isn't bringing out the best in you or the connection. Freedom and peace is also owning what you do need. It is important to acknowledge when someone is truly not good for us or bringing out the best in us.

Placing myself in positive relationships and environments for work and love has completely changed my life. People who want the best for you and support you by giving you their best self, not only change your outlook on life but also your sense of self. You will go from feeling like you're too much or not enough to realising you are just perfect and loved as you are. Go where you feel appreciated and are supported to shine, grow and evolve.

102

IF I LET GO OF MY ATTACHMENT, WHAT IS LOVE TEACHING ME

If we view love from a place of ascension and growth without attachment to a person, we open ourselves to seeing more clearly why they entered our life. Sometimes even why they had to leave.

Why did this person come into my life?

What did this person gift to me?

What did this person teach me about love?

What did they teach me about myself?

What did they bring out in me that I now see is important and something I will take forward with me?

What was the lesson I needed to learn here? And have I learnt it yet?

These are great journaling questions to ask yourself if you find yourself attached to a love that perhaps isn't bringing out the best in you and is more of a soulmate or karmic love. Every lesson learnt in love carries us forward on our soul life path. Closer to being in our fullest expression and in alignment with ourselves. Nearer to our one. But more importantly, ready for them.

103

WHAT WAS IT ABOUT THEM THAT MADE ME LOVE BEING AROUND

When we fall in love with, are we actually falling in love with is the feeling that they are bringing out in us and the way they make us feel. Yes, we are still in love with the person and their qualities, but it is the mutual energy of the two of you together when you are connecting that is pulling at your soul and psyche. Sometimes it is also what they open up within you. Allowing you to express and step into embodying a more brilliant version of yourself as a result of their love, attention and gaze, and loving you for it.

When a love leaves our life, whether this person returns to our life in time or not, this is the powerful reflection for us to have. What was it about them that made me love being around them? What did they bring out in me? How did I feel about myself when I was with them? The answers to these questions reveal the voids we can look to work on along our soul path. If someone made you feel sexy and desirable, can we not feel that way still without someone having to see that in us first? If they made you feel confident and good enough, can we not feel those things without someone choosing us and propping us up in those areas of self? The difference between a karmic love, the loves that we so easily find ourselves stuck in and repeating, and a higher love connection like a twin flame connection? Karmic soulmates are attracted to you when you're in a low vibration. Twin flames are attracted to you when you're in a high vibration or on the pathway to being so. Not perfectly healed or in alignment, but on the pathway to. Some of the greatest healing that we will go through is within these twin flame connections when they finally come into union in our life. When they go through the contrast of all of the stages of running, separation and coming together to clear our last final blocks and wounds away. The more we step into this higher vibration, the closer we move towards being ready for those beautiful higher connections to come into our life and to stay in our life. Not because they are karmic and oh so close but because they are our twin flame.

This love journey is ours to own. Keep walking, one step, one choice, one moment at a time. With every lesson, every act of self-love, and every step, we are becoming the women we were always meant to be. We are worthy of the kind of love that doesn't just enter our lives but stays. Because it is meant for us. Because we are ready. Because we have become the *queen of our own story*.

Acknowledgements

It is with my deepest personal and professional gratitude that I thank the coaches and shamans I have worked with since leaving my marriage in 2016. Your words and wisdom, shared in our sessions and time together, have energetically lifted me and elevated me onto my true path. Through your energetic imprint interwoven with my own, I have been able to shed all that I was not and to rise into the fullness of who I am, and who I was always meant to be. I have stepped into the woman I was destined to become, doing the work I am called to do today.

All of you have been invaluable in piecing together this puzzle of becoming myself, where fate, free will and destiny intertwine. With love and gratitude for your imprint upon me: Dave Blomsterberg, Tony Robbins, Claire Baker, Rori Raye, Julie Parker, Erica Lynn Carrico, Tracey Spencer, Ellie Swift, Ashae Sundara, Orion Shaman and Rhagida Shaman.

Learn more about Carla's coaching, programs, resources and products to make this next season of your life the best season of your life.

www.carladacosta.com

www.ingramcontent.com/pod-product-compliance
Lightning Source LLC
Chambersburg PA
CBHW060554080526
44585CB00013B/562